REFLECTIONS ON RIDING AND JUMPING

Also by William Steinkraus

Riding and Jumping

With M. A. Stoneridge

The Horse in Sport

As editor

Great Horses of the USET
The Complete Book of Show Jumping
The Encyclopedia of the Horse
The USET Book of Riding

REFLECTIONS ON RIDING AND JUMPING

Winning Techniques for Serious Riders

William Steinkraus

*Sequence Photographs by Alix Coleman
and Peter Winants*

Doubleday

New York   London   Toronto   Sydney   Auckland

PUBLISHED BY DOUBLEDAY
a division of Bantam Doubleday Dell Publishing Group, Inc.
666 Fifth Avenue, New York, New York 10103

DOUBLEDAY and the portrayal of an anchor with a dolphin
are trademarks of Doubleday,
a division of Bantam Doubleday Dell Publishing Group, Inc.

Library of Congress Cataloging-in-Publication Data

Steinkraus, William.
    Reflections on riding and jumping : winning techniques for serious
riders / by William Steinkraus ; sequence photographs by Alix Coleman
and Peter Winants.
        p.   cm.
    Includes bibliographical references.
    1. Show jumping.   2. Show riding.   I. Title.
SF295.5.S718   1991
799.2'4—dc20   90-40041
                                                                 CIP

ISBN 0-385-05162-X

BOOK DESIGN BY DONNA SINISGALLI

$\mathcal{T}$his book is gratefully dedicated to the many people who helped me in my riding career, and most especially to the memory of my mother and to my darling wife, without whose sacrifices my riding career would never have existed.

Acknowledgments

The author would like to acknowledge his appreciation of the generous collaboration of Alix Coleman and Peter Winants, who provided the photographs taken especially for this book, and to Bob Langrish, who supplied most of the others.

He would also like to thank *L'Année Hippique* for permission to reprint the final three chapters of this book, which originally appeared, in somewhat different form, in its pages.

Author's Note

The fact that riders and horses alike can be either male or female, and that many of us tend to refer to our horses as if they were human beings, can make books on riding that carefully observe these distinctions very awkward to read. In order to minimize this, I have arbitrarily referred to the rider as "he" throughout this book, and to the horse as "it," though I know perfectly well that there are many "she" riders, and ordinarily prefer to refer to horses, too, by gender. I beg the reader's indulgence (whatever his/her sex) for this treatment and hope that in practice the clarity gained justifies the imprecision.

Contents

PREFACE

*T*his is a book about riding—
and, in particular, about riding and training jumpers—by
someone who has been at it for over fifty years. So I am
not a beginner or a person whose theoretical knowledge
exceeds his practical experience. Neither do I have illu-
sions about my own omniscience; horses *always* have more
to teach us, as I am reminded anew every time I ride.
Nevertheless, it now seems the right time in my career to
sum up some considered opinions about this fascinating
activity.

In addressing this book to jumping riders, I use that
term in its broadest sense. Though I myself am usually

identified with show jumping, and many of my observations relate particularly to that activity, a jump is a jump, and what I have to say about show jumping is almost equally applicable to hunter riding, hunter seat equitation or what have you.

I am slightly chagrined that the ideas in this book, taken together, seem somewhat eclectic, instead of being rigorously and invariably "classical." But if classical is what I intuitively prefer, eclectic is what my own experience has taught me. A review of the influences that have shaped my development as a rider will quickly demonstrate why.

I started riding as a child with a wonderful Canadian-born lady of English extraction named Ada Maud Thompson (who, incidentally, founded the very first American branch of the British Pony Club in Wilton, Connecticut, in 1935). "Mrs. T." lived for fox hunting and thought it daft to jump big fences if hounds weren't running, in which case nothing could stop her. She was not much impressed by show jumpers as a group, but much admired the premier Army horseman Major (later General) Harry D. Chamberlin. She gave me his books to read as they originally appeared in the mid-1930s. Though I didn't realize it at the time, both she and Chamberlin were to have a profound influence on my life.

Gordon Wright got a crack at me next, long before there was any formal Fort Riley doctrine in his teaching. Gordon had a whole bunch of talented kids riding with him at that time, and he pitted us against each other, insulting us nonstop in his typically rough but good-natured way. We learned a lot from him, as well as from each other.

Next I came under the influence of the legendary Morton W. "Cappy" Smith, who ran a dealer's yard in a neighboring town. Cappy was then acknowledged to be the best jumper rider in the United States, and was certainly one of the most successful dealers of his generation. Riding for him was like having a famous professional as an older brother (or even an uncle, since the age gap between us was only ten years but the gap in authority was unbridgeable). Cappy had wonderful horses and a reason for everything, and he was so gifted that he could make it all work even when the reasons were suspect. The debt I owe him, both as a rider and as a person (for he did a lot to help me grow up), is incalculable.

During those same teenage years I got a bit of exposure to saddle-seat riding and driving under the tutelage of that fine horseman and great gentleman Frank J. Carroll, played a little stick and ball and a couple of practice polo matches at the old Blind Brook Polo Club (now the world headquarters for Pepsi-Cola!), and galloped racehorses for Arthur McCashin, later to become the first captain of the U.S. Equestrian Team and my lifelong friend.

The U.S. Army briefly taught me to ride all over again at Fort Riley in 1943, but the short course we got as enlisted men on our way overseas was a far cry from the comprehensive officers' course for which the Horsemanship Detachment was famous. We were soon walking behind mules in Burma anyway.

After World War II I was lucky enough to get some catch-riding opportunities and the chance to ride several different strings of nice horses for different people, all sadly no longer with us. These included "Prof." I. Q. Winters, Raymond Lutz, Arthur Nardin, Don Ferraro, and Eligio del Guercio, and the horses included such stars as Easy Winner, Trader Bedford, Trader Horn, Black Watch and Ping Pong, all of them capable of winning in any company in that era. I learned a lot from having to make most of the schooling and showing decisions for myself, and am eternally grateful to these generous people who expressed so much confidence in me so early in my career.

It was the Ferraros' Black Watch that earned me my first place on the infant "civilian" U.S. Equestrian Team in 1951, and after I made the team, another wonderful succession of owners were kind enough to entrust their horses to me to represent the United States. These included the late Samuel Magid, Mrs. John Wofford, Bernie Mann, Eleonora Sears, Walter Devereux and Gordon Wright; and also Sir John Galvin and his brilliant dressage rider daughter, Patricia, Bert Firestone, Patrick Butler, Kay Love and William D. Haggard III. The horses included Democrat, Hollandia, First Boy, Riviera Wonder, Saxon Wood,

Ksar d'Esprit, Blue Plum, Fire One, Unusual, Sinjon, Fleet Apple, Snowbound, Bold Minstrel and Main Spring. The only way you can choose among the horses in this group is to make a lot of qualifications! (And remember, as you read this list, what no rider should *ever* forget: *horses make riders.*)

During the twenty-odd years that I rode with the USET the prime influence on my riding was unquestionably the remarkable Hungarian-born cavalryman Bertalan de Némethy. Bert's early teaching derived largely from what had been instilled in him at the Hungarian and German cavalry schools—concepts to which I had previously had no exposure at all. But before long, he was developing variations of his own, perhaps influenced by the predominance of Thoroughbreds on our team. Of course, there were many other influences on me during those years, for the team experience gave me access to the ideas not only of our coaches for the other Olympic disciplines, but of my fellow competitors, both at home and abroad.

Thus, either through the USET or informally, I was able to study and closely observe the riding and training methods of several generations of brilliant horsemen, including but by no means limited to Richard Wätjen, Fritz Stecken and Josef Neckermann from West Germany; Bengt Ljunquist and Henri St. Cyr from Sweden; Hans Handler (and his son Michael), Franz Rochowansky, and Karl Mikolka of the Spanish Riding School of Vienna; Olympic gold medalists Hans Günter Winkler and Reiner Klimke, also from West Germany; Gunnar Andersen from Denmark; Harry Gilhuys from Holland; the USET's great Three-Day coach Jack Le Goff; Jean Saint-Fort Paillard from France's famed Cadre Noir at Saumur; the matchless d'Inzeo brothers, both extraordinarily interesting clinicians, from Italy; and innumerable good British riders, among them Jook and Robert Hall on the dressage side, and Harry Llewellyn, Pat Smythe, Ted Williams, Peter Robeson and David Broome among the jumpers.

I must confess unashamedly to having attempted to "borrow" from the example or precept of all the above (and many, many others as well) things that I could adopt or adapt for my own riding and training. I have also supplemented this "live" instruction with an extensive and extremely varied study of the marvelous literature of equestrian sport.

In sum, then, you can see why I have some reason to be fairly eclectic in my riding doctrines. The ideas I have ended up with are distilled from an effort to reconcile practices and principles drawn from all three main schools of Western equestrian thought—Anglo-American, Franco-Italian and German. Though this effort may not have been entirely free from a certain amount of confusion, I must say that I have found it far more fascinating than frustrating to compare different solutions to the age-old equestrian problems of lengthen, shorten, turn and jump. Now for a few disclaimers. I worry that some of my advice will not be very suitable for beginners, which is why my subtitle suggests that this is primarily a book for serious competitive riders. I haven't taught many real beginners, and have no idea how much they can absorb at first, even the most serious ones. So if you are a real beginner, maybe you'd be better off to put this book down and find a good beginners' teacher.

But maybe not. Because I have also wondered how anyone can learn what the good riders actually do if somebody doesn't tell them; I certainly wish that I had learned earlier in my riding career some of the ideas I finally grasped only after a great many false starts and a lot of trial and error. Because of these concerns, I have set down some practical advice in this book about things that are seldom discussed so frankly in print. And though I also still wonder if it is possible *fully* to grasp from the pages of a book techniques that one has not already started to figure out for one's self, I have often broken a dry spell in my own riding by trying an approach or method that I had never tried before. Indeed, if you get stuck on a particular problem, try asking all the good riders you know how they do it, and consult a good cross section of the serious books in your library. (Some of my own favorites are included in the Selected Bibliography at the end of this volume.) You may well get some fresh insights and at the very least, should get a consensus of conventional solutions, which can be quite helpful.

In the course of your studies, you may make the disillusioning discovery that not every teacher (or writer) tells you what he really thinks. Some seem to fear that if they tell you everything, you will know as much as they do and never come back. Others like to advise, "Do as I say, not as I do," though the chances are very good that if you want to achieve their results, you must use their *actual* methods.

This book may be somewhat unusual in that it describes very explicitly those methods that have worked best for me in practice and proven their usefulness over a long period of time. I am quite aware, of course, that they may not suit everyone as well as they suit me, and I would be the last person to discourage you from making your own experiments. But while every good rider must find his own way, to some extent, it is hard to learn very much if you have a closed mind, and I urge you to give my suggestions a fair trial.

If some of my ideas seem simplistic, especially in comparison with the complexity of their origins in many cases, I can only apologize and agree. Oddly enough, the most important principles of riding seem much simpler and more obvious to me today than they used to, perhaps because I don't have to cut corners in response to competitive pressure anymore. I'm happy to add that as my thinking about riding has become less complicated, I seem to get more out of more horses with less effort, and even greater pleasure from riding.

Observant readers may notice similarities between this book and an earlier work of mine, *Riding and Jumping,* which covers much of the same ground and employs the same basic approach. I am, after all, still the same person! However, this book was written entirely independently of the earlier one, and deals with a number of subjects that I touched on only lightly if at all in its predecessor. I could even say, as did the Duke of Newcastle of his second book, published in 1667, that it "may be of use without the other, as the other has been hitherto and still is, without this; but both together will questionless do best."

I hope that you will find this second book enjoyable as well as useful, and that it will help you to attain your own riding ambitions, whatever they may be.

W.S.

REFLECTIONS ON RIDING AND JUMPING

RATIONAL RIDING

*S*ince the idea of "rational rid-
ing" is an important underlying thesis of this book, it
might be useful if I started by explaining just what I mean
by this term. For me, rational riding is riding that depends on thought as well as feeling, on the brain as well
as the body. Of course, everyone considers his own riding
to be rational, and nobody has a monopoly on rationality.
Nonetheless, I know many wonderful "natural" riders who
apparently spend very little time planning what they are
going to do or trying to figure out why their horses continue to make the same mistakes. And that's great; hard as
they are to outride, the fact that you can outthink them

every now and then keeps things much more competitive. If the most gifted athletes in any sport worked as hard as some of those who are less richly endowed, they'd hardly ever be beaten.

Rational riding starts with the idea that it's easier to do something if you know very concretely *what* you're trying to do, *why* you're trying to do it and *how* it functions mechanically. "I can't work that way," some riders protest. "It leads to paralysis through analysis." Well, that's a good catch phrase, and it may even apply to some people, but there's another famous aphorism that is just as catchy and twice as valid: Those who can't learn from history are doomed to repeat it.

These days one hears and reads a lot about the distinction between teaching that emphasizes feeling and teaching that stresses mechanics, the implication often being that your training and methods should emphasize the way you most naturally incline. I beg to differ with this. My observation of half a century of great riders has shown me that they all had this in common: a reliable mechanical technique that, under the pressures of competition, they put at the service of their feeling, instinct, and sometimes even inspiration. I don't think it is possible to plan every detail of a great performance, nor do I think you can "feel" your way to it in the absence of a sound technique. You need to use all of your faculties. Hence, I believe that if you are a natural "feeler" your training must still include nuts and bolts and vice versa. It is important to exploit your virtues, but it is even more important to learn to compensate for your deficiencies.

It's especially important for weekend riders to understand what they're trying to do, for the lack of day-to-day continuity in their riding means that there will not be much natural carry-over of feeling. I know, for I have spent much of my life as a weekend rider! Of course, I tried to keep as much continuity going as I could. But for most of my twenty-odd-year career with the U.S. Equestrian Team, I was juggling my riding along with some form of "legitimate" gainful employment (as was required by the amateur code of that era), and my riding was often restricted to weekends and perhaps one very early morning in the middle of the week. Since the Team stables in New Jersey were quite a distance from my home in Connecticut, I usually spent almost as much time driving to and from the stables as I did riding. I occupied a lot of this commuting time in thinking about my horses—on my way out there, planning what I was going to try to accomplish, and on the drive back, reviewing what had happened, and what I wanted to work on the next time. In those days, I thought this was a considerable disadvantage, and that I'd have been much more competitive if only I could have ridden every day. But in retrospect, I think it may even have been an advantage, for over the years I learned to make better and better use of my time on horseback, and was able to think out possible solutions to problems that might never have occurred to me spontaneously.

Today I can't believe that every rider wouldn't benefit from spending some time consciously addressing his and his horses' strengths and weaknesses, and trying to find ways to exploit the former and correct the latter. In this connection, I often think of a story told me by the late Robert Hanson, the British transport magnate and MFH who owned a number of outstanding show jumpers and once had a son on the British team. Bob was a young apprentice in his father's transport firm early in World War I, when the company was providing horses to the British Army by the tens of thousands. Bob was dealing with some sort of difficult horse and getting nowhere, becoming madder and madder and rougher and rougher but with no visible effect on the horse, when his father's most senior horse "fixer" grabbed him by the scruff of the neck and made him stop. He was instructed to sit on a stool for thirty minutes, and to spend the time trying to figure out what the horse was thinking. Then he was to return to the horse and try whatever he wanted, provided that it was entirely different from what he had been doing.

Bob got the point that he had been acting without thinking, and relying on his very considerable brawn before engaging his brain. He returned to the horse after the half-hour's introspection and solved whatever the problem was in short order with little further fuss. He never forgot this episode, nor have I forgotten the image of this imposing personality sitting on a "dunce's" stool, learning to think his way out of problems!

Despite its emphasis on thinking, rational riding is still essentially pragmatic (responsive to the acid test of practical consequences) in that it is based on what works, rather than on what is theoretically supposed to be correct but *doesn't* work. Are you doing what you think is right, but the horse completely rejects it? And the more you persevere, the worse it gets? Then for heaven's sake, try something else!

One of the principal distinguishing characteristics of the good rider is his technical resourcefulness. If what he's doing isn't working, he'll try another approach until he finds something he can get by with, at least for the moment. They say of champion golfers that they learn how to score well even when they aren't playing well, and the same is true of good riders—they still produce useful performances even when they're not riding very well, or when their horses aren't in their best form. Thus it's always wise to have some other things to try if your horse seems to have gotten sick of what you've been doing. In fact, as a famous *écuyer* at Saumur has pointed out, it sometimes helps to try doing exactly the opposite. Perhaps you are using the wrong concept, or are executing the right one incorrectly or there is some other factor involved that you haven't thought about. And very often, it seems to me, diminishing returns are proof that you can exaggerate every virtue into a defect. (You will read more of this in Chapter 3, which deals with the rider's position.) Even excessive virtue can become obnoxious.

It's surprising what a big deal it is for most people actually to try something new. Thinking about it is one thing, but having to try it out on your own horse or with your own body means abandoning what you have always done before. Many riders can't bring themselves to do this, even when they're seeking advice in the first place because they aren't having much success with their old techniques. Every clinician has had the experience of describing and demonstrating a particular physical attitude he wants the class to assume, only to find that half the class isn't even attempting to do what he suggested. Consequently, most riders display the same faults year after year, their progress blocked by their own resistance to change, forever bogged down at a lower level of success than they are capable of achieving.

Rational riding is systematic and progressive. It attempts to create a sound foundation and then build upon it, step by step, proceeding from the simple to the more complex. Most of my teachers believed in this approach, which has also been implicit in much of my reading. (Harry Chamberlin, author of the first serious riding books I read, was also the principal architect of the U.S. Cavalry School manual, which is nothing if not methodical, as Army manuals tend to be.)

Surprisingly, perhaps, my belief in this approach has been reinforced by my musical experience. People who know that I love music and still play the viola or violin almost every day have often asked me if there was any relationship between my musical activities and my riding. They probably expect me to say something about hands or rhythm; but I've never found these things to have much direct relevance *per se*. What has been relevant, however, is the relationship between position and function, and especially, the method of practicing difficult technical material by isolating all the elements involved, reducing them to their simplest terms, and learning to cope with them on that level before putting everything back together. To master a very difficult passage on the violin, fiddle players often practice the actions required by the bow arm and the left hand separately, and invent little *ad hoc* exercises that accentuate the particular patterns involved. Then they go back to the passage and practice it in slow motion, to give the correct neural paths a chance a establish themselves; and when they finally play the passage at the proper tempo, it's all there—not miraculously, but mechanically.

Difficult riding problems can be dealt with in exactly the same way. The key to a demanding Grand Prix jumper course is often a particular difficult line involving big fences, difficult distances, a combination and a turn that must be executed with great precision. Yet each of these elements can be isolated and mastered in simpler form in schooling long before we face them all together and in a more complex version during competition. For example, we can work out the line and the turn by using simple rails on the ground or cavalletti at the trot and canter; we can work out the distance problems of the combination through cavalletti and gymnastic grids. And when we put all these ingredients back together at speed over big fences, we can handle the problem instead of being overwhelmed by its difficulty and complexity.

Thus I'm convinced that sound riding instruction and horse training must, like good musical training, be progressive, starting with a mastery of fundamentals and adding complexity only as the pupil is ready to cope with it. Even though your goal may be a dazzling performance of the Tchaikovsky Violin Concerto, you must still start by mastering open strings and "Twinkle, Twinkle, Little Star." And even though your goal may be the Olympic Games, you will have little chance of achieving it unless you and your horse have mastered your own kinds of fundamentals— work without stirrups, flat work, cavalletti and gymnastic exercises—just as thoroughly. You will find detailed discussions of all of these ingredients in the chapters that follow.

Despite the emphasis in this chapter on thinking about riding, and reading about it, I freely concede that you can't ultimately learn to ride anywhere but on a horse. I do believe, however, that it is much easier to *think* your way to feeling than it is to *feel* your way to thinking. You need to do both if you want to succeed these days: nothing less will do.

Two

EQUIPPING YOURSELF FOR RIDING

celebrated recipe for rabbit stew starts with the sensible advice, "First, you have to get a rabbit." It is equally true that to be a rider, first you need a horse.

It may be rented, borrowed or purchased (I'd stop short of stealing), and it certainly need not be a "fancy" horse. In fact, if you are just starting out, too fancy a horse can be a hindrance rather than a help, and many riders who are overmounted at the start never develop normally. The main thing is to have a healthy, sound, more or less normal horse; such a horse can be taught a lot and can teach you a lot in return. In conducting clinics and on various hunting trips I have ridden a wide variety of "ordinary" horses, all of which were interesting in one way or other, and most of which were really fun to ride. The idea that you have to mortgage the homestead to buy a world-beater before you can have fun on horseback or realize your potential as a rider is sheer nonsense.

In Chapter 12 you will find more detailed advice on different kinds of horses and what to look for in a jumper, but for now I will insist only on the most fundamental preconditions: first, you have to get a horse. And just as riders come in any sex, age, shape or size, so do horses. It won't hurt if there is a certain minimal suitability between the two of you; tall, string-bean riders look and feel pretty funny on short, fat ponies! If you are interested in jumping, it is important for the horse to have enough ability to cope with the size of fences required at your competitive level, and if possible, a little extra scope beyond what is absolutely essential. This is your insurance policy for those times when you don't get to the fence exactly as you planned.

At the beginning of your riding career, your saddlery will usually be supplied by the riding academy or stable that provides the horse and your instruction, and your clothing may be pretty rudimentary. Blue jeans are hardly ideal, but many novice riders make do with them. In fact, if you combine them with a pair of jodhpur shoes or paddock boots and leather "schooling chaps" you will be dressed just as 90 percent of "English" riders dress 90 percent of the time and will look like an accomplished rider well before you can perform like one.

For shows, of course, you need to be more conventionally attired, and some stubbornly old-fashioned riders like myself still prefer even to school or exercise in boots and breeches, feeling that you can ride just a little better with them and owe your horse the best you've got. Some teachers also insist that their pupils wear jodhpurs or boots and breeches because it's sometimes hard to see just what the leg is doing in chaps. Chances are that you'll look at what everyone else is doing in your particular environment, and then pick the style that suits your own taste and personality. The local tack shop can give you a good idea of your range of options, and if you don't have one within easy reach, you can always use one of the big mail-order catalogues, which offer a wide range of products in every quality and price range.

When you get around to owning your own saddle (and you will not be happy until you do) the same sources will serve you again. The oldest, soundest advice about saddlery or tack is to buy the best you can afford and care for it scrupulously. Be sure to look around, however, and to try a lot of different saddles before you decide what you want to invest in. Saddles with a lot of "features" often appeal to the novice who hopes that the saddle will create his seat for him, but unfortunately it doesn't work out that way.

My own ideas about saddles are embodied in the Hermès that I designed many years ago, which I continue to find entirely satisfactory. However, I'm only of average size, and can imagine that someone much larger or smaller might prefer something else. You never can tell how you'll like a saddle, and how it fits you, until you've ridden in it, and it's worth taking the trouble to borrow a saddle from someone who already owns what you think you might like before you invest. Sitting on it on the showroom wooden rack isn't the same at all. New saddles can also be deceptive, since it's hard to guess how they'll break in. I wouldn't hesitate to buy a sound secondhand saddle and thus know exactly what I was getting. Though dealers may be reluctant to let you try a brand-new saddle, they will usually let you take a secondhand saddle on trial.

While saddles are a matter of individual taste (after all, it's your fanny) I do have a few personal opinions: It is *essential* that the lowest point in the seat is halfway between the pommel and the cantle and not further back, which makes you feel as if you're always riding slightly uphill; the head or pommel must not press against the top of the withers of a horse of average conformation (if it does, it's more often because the tree is spread than because of bad original design, but I've seen the latter, too); flaps and skirts must be heavy enough to resist folding or curling up under your leg; finally, the stirrup bars must hold the stirrup leathers securely *with the safety latch open* (and it should *never* be closed!).

My final advice, in saddlery as in everything else, is simply to avoid excess. The seat shouldn't be too flat or too deep, nor the panels so overstuffed that you are lifted high off the horse's back, nor the knee rolls so large that your freedom of movement is limited.

You should also avoid extremes in your choice of gloves, whip and spurs. Gloves should combine warmth or ventilation, as required, with lack of bulk; but even summer gloves should not be so light that they offer little protection and wear out easily. Riding gloves should either have their seams turned in where the reins go, be protected by an additional layer, or both. Whips should be long enough and stiff enough for the horse to know when you hit it, but should not be bludgeons, limp noodles or toys. Anything is better than hitting a horse with your hand, however, and every horse must learn to accept the fact that you are going to carry a stick. It is important to have a stick that is well balanced and comfortable to carry, since you will spend much more time carrying it than you ever will spend hitting with it. And remember, the hitting you do is intended to surprise and embarrass the horse more than to inflict pain, so the whip should have a broad, "popper" kind of keeper, and not be so thin that it can easily mark a horse.

It is hard to find whips of a convenient length. Very long ones tend to catch the corner of the horse's extensive peripheral vision, while very short ones are hard to carry (since they don't rest against your leg in the right way) and are almost useless as a riding aid. To get one I like, I have often assembled my own from various components.

In addition to your regular stick, it is useful to have a long dressage whip, for use only on the flat. With a little practice you can become adept at administering just the right amount of touch or tap with such a whip without removing your hand from the reins, and this can be very useful in encouraging horses to change behind when they are learning to make flying changes, for example, and in starting half-passes. It is not a bad idea to get into the habit of always carrying your whip in the inside hand, as is *de rigueur* at the Spanish Riding School, since this is ordinarily the side from which you will want to use it.

Short, dull spurs are all that many thin-skinned horses require or will tolerate. But you should also have a hammerhead pattern with its sharp corner, to use with horses that are able to ignore the dull spur; and maybe also a pair with longer shanks, if your legs are very long. (I am assuming, of course, that your leg is sufficiently educated for you to be wearing spurs in the first place.) Most advanced riders will also want to own a pair of dull roweled spurs to alert the attention of very sluggish horses, although many real experts do without them. In any case, no good horseman uses a spur that could cut a horse. Moderation is the rule, especially here. I myself usually wear spurs as a matter of course, except with the occasional horse (more often mare) that is so abnormally sensitive to leg aids that any spur at all would be too much. In such cases, I usually defer to the animal's preference.

It goes without saying that all of your riding clothing and equipment should be horsemanlike. But it is just as important that you really like it. You'll never ride well in a saddle you hate. Neither will you be able to ride well if the skin on your fingers, legs or seat bones is chafed or torn, or if your underwear is cutting you in two, or if it provides inadequate support. Thanks to stretch materials, it's now possible to avoid these agonies almost entirely. Knees can be particularly troublesome for the jumping rider, for once they get torn up they never have a chance to heal. I often used to apply a protective patch of adhesive elastic bandage to my knees before the start of every show, especially during hot weather, and found it much easier to try to avoid opening up the skin on my knees than to deal with it later.

Hard hats are now required under both national (AHSA) and international (FEI) rules for all jumping, both in and out of the show ring, and it behooves you to find the best trade-off you can between comfort and protection. Though early efforts to develop helmets and harnesses that are comfortable, attractive and still offer adequate protection have been disappointing, hope springs eternal, and I pray that some truly satisfactory solutions will soon evolve. For until they do, compliance with the rules will tend to remain a problem. As long as the only hard hats that meet statutory requirements are ugly, uncomfortable or both, many riders will attempt to go without them whenever they think they can get away with it, even though the consequences may prove tragic.

My best general advice about all your essential items of clothing and equipment is to shop about, trade and experiment until you have assembled a set of things that suit your taste and that you find effective as well as comfortable. Take good care of these articles so that when you are riding you can forget about them. Whether you are showing or only training, your mind must always be free to concentrate on how your horse is going, how you are riding, the course and the other truly important things.

It would probably be most logical to conclude this discussion of tack and equipment with some remarks about bits, bridles and related appurtenances. However, this is a big subject that I am loathe to deal with only briefly and superficially, and it is not really essential to the major theses of this book. Accordingly, I have dealt with it separately in a chapter all its own starting on page 135. Instead, I would now like to deal with the only really necessary part of the rider's wherewithal that we have not yet touched upon: some form of instruction.

Even though I'm a confirmed do-it-yourselfer in most things, and one who believes that you never fully mature as a rider until you accept full responsibility for the riding and training of your own horses, I'd be the last to suggest that you can get by without good instruction in the earlier stages of your riding education, or that a perceptive coach, ground man or critic is not invaluable at all stages of your career. In other words, if you do something wrong it is not the horse's fault or your instructor's fault—it is your fault. But the knowledge and experience of a competent teacher can save you countless false starts and dead ends and enormously accelerate your development as a rider.

Some years ago I read in the *New York Times* the summary of a Ph.D. thesis that sought to establish common denominators in the development of world-class swimmers (teenagers) and prodigy pianists of the same age. It concluded that there were indeed common factors. The parents, while not necessarily involved in the particular activity themselves, had to be supportive, and the family "work-ethic" oriented. The child had to start young, and with a teacher who was known to be good with children though not necessarily very advanced technically. The second teacher had to be a very sound technician; the third teacher, world-class. And the child had to get to the third teacher while still fifteen or sixteen.

This progression seems to me to be very natural. Not many top-class teachers take much interest in beginners, and teachers who go very much by the book are often reluctant to let their pupils express much individuality. I think it is also valid for many other activities, (riding among them) and is, in fact, also a pretty good curriculum for a talented horse: it should be broken by someone who is excellent with young horses, brought along by a rider who has solid training basics and finally shown by a gifted show rider. There are very few horsemen who can accomplish all three stages with equal skill.

What should you look for in your own teacher(s)? First of all, the proven ability to turn out the kind of rider you want to be, whether that is a local equitation winner, a Grand Prix rider or simply an enthusiastic, improving adult beginner. (Of course, your immediate goals have to bear some relationship to reality, and the higher you aim the more tortuous the road.) Next, you should seek compatibility. Though the traditional image depicts the riding master as a martinet, you should not only be able to get along well with your teacher, but really like and respect him. Word of mouth and reputation are the best references, but if you can also audit a lesson or a class to estimate how your own "chemistry" might work with a particular individual, so much the better. You'll never make much progress with a teacher you resent, dislike or find unsympathetic. Ideally, you should enroll with one whose basic approach you can understand and whose basic physical build is not too different from your own. After all, a teacher can teach only what he knows, based on his own riding and teaching experience. If you are five feet two and he measures six feet three, he's likely to have less insight into some of your riding problems than someone who is five feet six. (I know that with my relatively long legs I can do things that shorter-legged riders cannot do, and surely a long upper body must feel quite different from one that's more compact.)

Once you've learned all you can absorb from any particular teacher, you must recognize as objectively as possible when the time has come to move on to a different one. This will not be easy, for if finding a teacher can be hard, leaving one can be even harder! Nonetheless, you must try to recognize the point at which you need somebody with a different approach or a different way of expressing things to solve some of your old problems and push you onto a higher level. And of course, you also ought to be able to learn something from studying with or watching any good horseman, as well as from reading anything written by those whose experience and success give their views unquestionable validity. Indeed, if you are lucky, you will continue to learn from your different human teachers as well as from your horses throughout your entire riding career.

Three

THE RIDER'S POSITION

*F*or most riders, details of position are awfully boring. Why, then, devote a whole chapter to them? Because the kind of riding I'm talking about is more than simply staying on. It inevitably involves the education and development of the horse, and this is accomplished through our aids—our body language—by eliciting and rewarding the behavior we want, and by resisting and blocking the behavior we do *not* want. And in order to resist, sustain and reward effectively, our aids must be totally independent of the business of staying on, and they must function from a stable platform. That platform is our position, or more precisely, *those* positions that facilitate the instrumental acts we require. Since these instrumental acts will vary according to whether we need to sustain, reward, resist or even protect ourselves, it follows that our basic position should be a median one, from which we can readily shift into all of the other positions we may wish or need to assume.

Rewarding usually means yielding or following. Sustaining usually means gently supporting. And resisting usually means fixing or bracing. We fix, brace or resist with most of our musculature by flexing. We yield by extending; and we sustain by assuming an essentially neutral position midway between the two. The basic position I'll describe is one in which most joints and muscles have the widest range of motion in either direction, as well as the most elasticity, which is approximately halfway between flexion and extension.

I take pains to explain all of this because I think that if you really understand the reasons for something, you are much less likely to forget it than if you have merely learned it by rote. Moreover, I don't want you to try what I suggest simply because I say so; I want you to try it because it makes sense to you. The bottom line is really very simple: if you sit wrong, it's hard to ride right. Form and function in riding (as in everything else) are intimately related, and as boring as a detailed discussion of the rider's various positions may be for some, a thorough understanding of the subject is fundamental and essential.

Before you can assume any position on horseback at all you must mount up. But even before you mount, you must remember to inspect the horse and its tack to verify that everything is correct. Someone else may own the horse, someone else may be responsible for its care, feeding and grooming and someone else may have tacked it up for you, but if *you* are going to ride it, the final responsibility is yours. Do the feet, legs and general expression seem all right? Is the bit properly adjusted, and are the keepers on the bridle all in place? Is the martingale adjustment correct? Is the saddle pad in place, and is there a pommel pad, if one is needed? Is the girth untwisted, and sufficiently tight for you to mount? Every rider must run down all these questions in his mind every time he gets on a horse, for doing so can avoid a lot of grief—and "I didn't notice" is no excuse.

If you're tall enough, I think it's a good idea to make a habit of always getting up from the ground, instead of asking for a leg up or using a mounting block. You never know when the skill will come in handy. (And unused skills eventually atrophy.) I'm only five feet ten, but still can cope with horses up to seventeen hands. Having relatively long arms, I like to reach across the seat with my right hand, to minimize turning the saddle. My left hand grasps the horse's neck just in front of the withers, with the off rein held a little shorter than the other. An advantage of this method is that if the horse takes a step, its shoulder will move into you instead of away.

While we're at it, we may as well discuss dismounting, because I think there's also a better and a worse way to accomplish this. Many authorities recommend removing your right foot from the stirrup, swinging it over the horse's back and then supporting yourself in the left stirrup for a moment before descending to the ground. Personally, I much prefer to remove both feet from the stirrups and then, placing my right hand on the pommel and my left in front of the withers, jump down in one move. I've seen too many accidents and near-accidents occur when riders got stuck halfway down, or changed their minds when the horse moved, and tried to get back on. Once you make up your mind to get off, *do* it. And do it all at once.

A SPECTRUM OF SEATS

Every rider needs not one, but a whole collection of seats suitable for the particular range of equestrian activities in which he may participate, as well as the variations of each one. My own basic hunter/jumper seat is therefore simply a neutral seat, located somewhere near the middle of the whole spectrum that the hunter/jumper rider needs.

At one extreme of the spectrum is the highly defensive "safety" seat, a seat from which the rider cannot possibly fall off forward; at the other is the highly permissive, extreme forward seat, with which the rider can readily encourage his horse's forward movement in a passive way, but otherwise has little influence. In the first seat, the rider is very much behind the horse; in the second, somewhat ahead of it. But each seat has its uses, and the rider needs to have access to both of them, especially in their more moderate forms. The position from which he can most readily adapt to every variation is what I'll call "the Median Seat."

I hasten to add that having a whole collection of seats, including some extreme ones, doesn't mean that you use all of them every day. Quite the contrary! In fact, if we arbitrarily say that the median seat is situated at 5.0 on a scale from 0 to 10, most of your riding will be in the area from 4.8 to 5.2 and only rarely make an excursion into something more extreme.

The Median Seat

The median seat is not only halfway between an extreme forward seat and an extreme backward seat; it is also median in the sense that most of the rider's joints and muscles are in a median position, halfway between the extremes of full extension and complete flexion. In this neutral position, they not only enjoy maximum elasticity, but at the same time can move very readily in either direction. Let's examine this position in detail, starting from the bottom:

I like to see the rider simply "carry" his toe, so that it is only slightly higher than the heel, with the ball of the foot resting on the inside of the tread of the stirrup iron. From this position the rider can either raise the heel, in order to apply it or a spur very accurately, or lower it, in order to absorb shock or intentionally harden the calf for added drive or security. It's important to remember that even a virtue, carried to excess, may become a sin. So it is with the deep heel. If the heel is forced as low as it will go, the ankle will be frozen shut, no longer able to function as a spring; while the calf in full extension loses its elasticity and becomes impossible for a sensitive horse to accept. (Some teachers and equitation judges cannot imagine too deep a heel, but I still regard it as functionally wrong.) The toe should turn out only to the extent that it normally does in walking.

The bottom of the calf should be applied to the little triangle of the horse's side just behind the girth and just below the saddle flap, if the rider's leg is long enough. Ideally, this is the place where you add or subtract calf pressure in order to modulate your driving aids. If you like to think of having a bolt driven through your legs to create a secure, stable seat, that is where you should visualize it, and not through the knee. If you do so, you will never pinch with the knee, and never have a problem in posting too high or assuming too high a half-seat. (I prefer the term "half-seat" for what is sometimes called a "two-point" position.) When the heel is not excessively deep, the calf itself will be elastic and clinging. Leveling the foot more makes it even softer for horses that try to reject the leg. Dropping the heel hardens the calf as needed in emergencies or for drive.

The knee should be placed, rather than forced, against the saddle. A "pinched" knee on which the rider pivots invariably leads to an unstable or swinging lower leg. (The fact that some very expert riders have a swinging lower leg in the air while jumping doesn't mean that it isn't a fault. They'd probably do even better if they corrected it.) In fact, a feeling that the knee is open is far preferable to the feeling that you are catching all of the weight of your upper body on your knee, or trying to drive weight down into your heels. To ride well, which is to say, to have maximum influence over your horse, you must learn to ride through the balance and erectness of the upper body; and if you are taking a lot of weight in your heels, knees or thighs, that weight cannot be falling into your seat bones, supported by the buttocks, as it should be. Trying to *lighten* your thighs is therefore a very useful exercise. The great thing about riding with weight and balance is that it requires little strength, since weight is an inherent quality that cannot suffer from fatigue or strain as muscles and tendons do.

The hip angle is a function of the combined attitudes of the thigh and pelvis, and is therefore dependent on the length of stirrup. In a normal seat, I believe that the pelvis should be almost exactly vertical, so that it can readily tip slightly backward (for drive) or forward (for accompanying the horse's forward motion).

Most riders find it easier to straighten their pelvis if they think of "tucking in their tail feathers," while the opposite feeling—sticking your fanny out—tends to characterize a hollow-backed position.

Perhaps the crucial point in dealing with the rider's seat is the attitude of the back or spinal column. You must be able to release your back vertically, so it can swing freely with the horse's back, and you also must be able to stress or brace it readily. I'd say that the back is in its neutral or median position when it *feels* straight, although it is really in a very shallow S-curve. A good way to assume this position is simply to stretch up, lifting your chest up from the pelvic basin. Riders who habitually stand and sit hollow-backed may need to flex (round) their backs first, while keeping their shoulders erect, in order to support the small of the back. Otherwise they will tend to overextend the back, and place it in a C-curved position from which it cannot possibly swing freely.

If the shoulders are comfortably drawn back (never rounded or hunched forward), the head will naturally be free, easy and erect as well. The eyes should be focused on where you're going, a simple thing that seems to help coordinate all of the rider's actions on horseback. (If you have to look down to check a lead or a diagonal, learn to do it without inclining your head.) Looking where you're going is especially important in turning: if you look directly at your ultimate objective, you'll make a much better turn. But you don't have to snap your head around, as some equitation riders get into the habit of doing, in order to accomplish this.

Another critically important aspect of the rider's position is the attitude of his arms and hands, because of the intimate relationship between their position and function.

What must the hand and arm be able to do? Yield, sustain, resist. What they do *not* need to do is pull, because no rider has ever won a pulling contest with a horse. In order to sustain and resist, the hands must be supported from the rider's elastically braced back and, to the necessary degree, from the support of the upper arm against the side. To yield, the elbow joint must be able to open. In view of these functions, a forced, low, flat hand, with the palm facing the horse's shoulder and the elbow joint fully extended, is distinctly *un*functional, even though it is very common.

In the past, many riding instructors used to make their pupils ride with sticks or whips held in their armpits. Perhaps, as has been claimed, this exercise produced a certain stiffness. But it is a surefire remedy for the hopelessly ineffective "bear hug" position of the arms, with the elbows miles away from the body; and it certainly forces the rider to learn what it feels like to support the upper arm with his body. And unless you can find this support, you'll never really be able to "fix" the hand.

For me, the hands and arms are in a correct neutral position only if the upper arm falls almost vertically from the shoulder joint, the elbow falling just slightly in front of the hip, with which it should feel a sort of elastic connection. The line from the elbow to the horse's mouth should be essentially straight (or with the hand just an inch higher, at most), which in turn will make an angle of almost ninety degrees in the elbow joint, placing the hands two or three inches in front of the pommel of the saddle, just past the mid-point of the withers, and a couple of inches higher.

The hands themselves may be used functionally in any attitude from palms completely down (which releases the elbows from the rider's side) to palms facing your own eyes (which is an extremely powerful position from which to resist a horse that is attempting to force your hand). Thus the neutral or median position is one in which the hands are at an angle between thirty and forty-five degrees from the vertical (usually closer to vertical than flat), and separated by two to six inches, depending on the degree to which the rider wishes to urge the horse forward or to inhibit its forward movement. (The more widely you separate your hands, the more you encourage the horse to enter the "corridor" they form.)

You can recognize from what I've said above why I find the position of the rider's arms with flat hands and an extended elbow such an impediment to good riding. The fact that the hands are forced forward and low rounds the rider's shoulders, pulls his buttocks out of the saddle and shifts his weight too far forward; the fact that the elbow is extended robs him of the use of that joint as a means of insulating the hands from the movement of the upper body (in the posting trot, for example), and encourages him both to pull and to rest his hands on the horse's mouth. ("You must make a contract with your horse," Commandant Licart of the Cadre Noir liked to say. "He carries his head, and you carry your hands.")

The correct seat is often described as one in which the head, hips and heels are in the same vertical plane, and this is, in fact, the *feeling* you should have. If you feel that your heels are drawn back to where they can support the hips, and that you could easily assume a half-seat without changing anything else very much, you will be sitting pretty well. Often, however, the photo illustrating the "head, hips and heels" advice contradicts it to some extent, because actually following the advice requires a rider with long legs and rather short stirrups. Most of the time, a vertical line dropped from the rider's head and passing through his hips will fall somewhat *behind* the heel, which is not only acceptable, but correct.

So much for the median seat. Let's proceed to the more extreme seats that a good rider should also possess if he is to cope with every eventuality. To start with, there are those that can help him survive emergency situations:

The Defensive Seats

All seats in which the rider's center of gravity is placed somewhat behind that of the horse, with the leg pushed forward and the small of the back more or less convex (rounded), belong to the defensive end of the spectrum. Defensive seats enable the rider to influence the horse by resisting as well as by driving it forward. Their disadvantage is that they make it difficult to accompany the horse smoothly in its forward movement.

The purest form of defensive seat is probably that of a rodeo bronc rider in the chute or at the bottom of a buck-jump: his legs are straight, along the line of the horse's shoulder, while his own shoulders may even touch the horse's croup. A more practical defensive seat is the one used by Three-Day Event riders for the cross-country phase, or by hunt race riders in the Maryland Hunt Cup. The toe is still "cocked," but the upper body is more erect. What these riders do is not "wrong"—it is right and necessary for these particular activities.

What about the average rider? Does he ever really need a "safety" seat? He certainly does! (Though hopefully, not all the time.) But because he *really* needs it when he does need it, he should never be so far committed toward the opposite extreme in his basic seat that he cannot readily assume a safety seat. It may save him a trip to the hospital or a long walk home!

You need a strong defensive seat with any horse that is reluctant to go forward, that shies, wheels, bucks or rears; with any horse that is in danger of falling for whatever reason (leaving out a stride when it's not "on," or adding one in the approach to a fence); and with any horse one is attempting to resist defiantly. No matter how elegant your neutral seat and your forward seat may be, you'll never be a good rider if you don't also have a reliable collection of defensive seats. In fact, the very best riders usually have a hint of defensiveness in their ordinary, neutral seat, and always ride just a bit "behind the motion," as some teachers term it. They elicit the horse's movement and go along with it when it comes. They never initiate a movement with their own body in the hope that it will synchronize with a movement the horse is making or that the horse will catch up with them.

The Forward Seats

All of the seats that feature short stirrups and forward inclination of the body are forward seats. Popularized by an Italian cavalry officer, Captain Federico Caprilli, just after the turn of the century, they revolutionized cross-country riding and made possible modern show jumping. Before Caprilli's time, the emphasis had been almost entirely on high jumping and broad jumping, and the dominant seat, even for jumping, was somewhere in between the dressage seat and what I have described above as an extreme defensive seat. It was not until forward riding was adopted that the jumping horse was really free enough to demonstrate its innate capabilities.

However, even the very great virtues of the forward seat are susceptible to exaggeration, and the more artificially "perched" versions are of limited usefulness. They are wonderful for riding a free-going, "made" horse around a low hunter or jumper course; the rider exerts little effort to stay with his horse in the air, because he maintains the jumping position even at a standstill. But a determined horse can easily tip the extreme forward seat rider so far in front of its own center of gravity that the rider can neither effectively drive nor resist. I'd hate to try to ride a young horse, or go fox hunting in trappy country, or cope with a nappy horse, or even ride a nice horse for very many hours in such a seat. It's hard to influence a horse effectively if you don't have any contact with it through your seat, and in the more extreme versions of the forward seat the rider never really sits. For the rider who doesn't know what it's like to get off his own tail, however, this feeling can open up a whole new world. Besides, getting a taste of an opposite extreme can often be a useful step in expanding one's technical resources.

The Rider's Position at Various Gaits

So far I've described the rider's seats almost as if they were static positions, but riding is essentially a motive sport. So let's consider now how your position should function when the horse is moving at various gaits.

Walk

Basically, the median position I have described remains unchanged at the walk. However, the forward and backward movement of the horse's head require the rider's elbow joint to open and close slightly in rhythm with the horse's gait, and the rider's body to move freely inside the arms if perfect contact with the mouth is to be maintained. Novice riders, with their extended elbows and flat hands, find this impossible; and the intermittent contact that results says to the horse: "I don't ride very well yet." Even at the walk, the horse's forward movement must be supplely supported from behind. A slight lateral swing of the horse's belly at the walk suggests the right tempo of slight alternating pressures by the rider's calves, which need only accept or contain this movement.

Posting Trot

All of the various posting trots—collected, working (or ordinary), medium and extended—require a somewhat shorter rein, a slight forward inclination of the body and a bit more support from behind. The key to the posting trot is that the only work the rider does is to synchronize his return to the saddle with the horse's gait; he insists on the horse doing the work of throwing him up, and if the trot has insufficient energy to do this, he sits to the trot instead.

Posting is *not* a matter of pushing yourself up and sitting back down. It's a matter of letting the horse throw you up and of controlling your descent. In this way, it's either the horse or the force of gravity that provides most of the energy.

At slower trots, it is important to post "cleanly," that is, with no trace of a double bounce. At faster trots, it is important not to post too high, which is much facilitated if you make your pivot point the lower calf instead of the knee. When you pivot on the knee, a fresh, strong horse will find it easy to tip you even further forward and "take" you at the trot. The answer to this is to refuse to accept much weight in your knees, and to push your pelvis forward as you return to the saddle, thus maintaining the relative erectness of your upper body. You should feel that the knee moves forward and down as you return to the

saddle, and that you're returning your seat to the exact
center of the saddle, or even to a point further toward the
pommel—never toward the cantle.

As at the walk, an opening and closing of the elbow
joint is essential to maintaining a stable hand and even
contact with the horse's mouth. The most common faults
at the posting trot are posting too high and from front to
back (that is, with the pelvis coming forward as it rises,
and moving back toward the cantle as the rider sits), reins
that are too long and hands that rise and fall as the body
rises and falls.

The Sitting Trot

Many riders think a good sitting trot is some sort of
divine gift, and fail to master it even after years of painful
practice. Others maintain that the only way to acquire it is
to spend months on the longe line without stirrups or
reins. (This does, in fact, work in most cases, if only because pain and fatigue eventually force you to find the
natural correct way, which is a function of balance and
controlled relaxation.) What you're really trying to do in a
good sitting trot is to "sit down and rest," as a noted
dressage coach puts it. No sitting trot is any good if there
isn't absolute adherence between the buttocks and the
saddle, with no bouncing and no concussion. In order to
produce a good one, the back must be elastic enough to
absorb the natural concussion of the horse's gait, and the
rider must find a balance that permits him to release his
back to the appropriate extent.

This balance is always found from behind. No living
human being can perform an acceptable sitting trot with
his shoulders tipped forward and his pelvis back in relation to them. In such a posture, you can only fake it, by
never really sitting on the horse's back. (Watch any equitation class and you'll see what I mean!) Many teachers
tell you to "sit *up*"; but the real key is to sit with your
shoulders *behind* your pelvis, with your pelvis as far *forward*
as possible (because the point at which the horse's long
back muscles insert into its shoulders is the point at which
they have the minimum amplitude of motion), and with
your back soft or even slightly rounded. If this doesn't

work, exaggerate the same posture until you find the feeling of "getting with" the horse and being able to accompany its movements. Only then can you finally "sit up," support your back and assume a more erect posture while still following the horse's movement. But unless you have the feeling of moving up to this position from behind, you'll never make it. If you start with your basic balance too far forward and your pelvis also tipped forward, it's almost impossible to work back to the position in which you can find the correct balance.

Canter

For the various kinds of canter in a full seat, you'll again have to shorten your reins somewhat in order to keep your hands in the correct position relative to your body and to the horse's withers. The commonest problems in cantering are primarily those of balance and consequent inability to sit without rolling, bouncing or cheating. Again, the solution lies in pushing the pelvis forward relative to the shoulders, and being sufficiently erect and balanced to release your back and really sit. Bad or ineffective riders simply roll or post even to a short, slow canter and cannot move the horse from behind, so that it's always cantering on its forehand. This often happens because the reins are so short that they pull the rider's shoulders forward, tipping the pelvis at the same time. The right feeling is quite different. Once again, it's a feeling of pushing the pelvis forward relative to the shoulders, letting the body work inside the arms instead of being blocked by them, and riding the horse from behind into a long rein through the elastic support of a soft back.

The Hand-Gallop and Gallop

While a half-seat is appropriate for these gaits, (the so-called "two-point" position), I still like a *clean* half-seat, in other words, one without any posting. It may be true that some good riders emulate the cowboys by more or less posting to the canter, and they may look pretty good doing it. But that's because their basic balance is correct and because they're riding the horse from behind into a long rein.

Incidentally, I used to think all that British talk about a "lovely long rein" was rather silly, but there's a certain element of truth in it. You can't ride with a long rein unless you're moving the horse from behind and sitting in the middle of the horse. Even leading jockeys (such as Bill Shoemaker, one of the all-time best) have never needed to strangle a horse to get it to run over a distance of ground.

As at the other gaits, if you feel you're getting "tippy" and losing your balance to the front, simply push forward with your pelvis, and let your knees move forward and down. If you're riding a "puller," make it pull against your pelvis rather than your shoulders and arms, and keep your upper body sufficiently erect to let some of its weight filter through your fingers.

Managing the Reins

Managing the reins may seem a simple subject, but when teaching clinics I've been struck by the number of riders who hold the reins incorrectly, have little facility in adjusting them and consistently ride with the wrong length of rein. It's most often too short, so that their shoulders are pulled too far forward; but sometimes it's too long, so that there is only intermittent contact with the horse's mouth.

For me, there's only one way to hold a single snaffle rein: fixed between the thumb and index finger (more precisely, at the second phalange, next to the tip), and exiting from the hand between the ring finger and the little finger. The rein is held by the thumb, which acts as a sort of set screw, and is manipulated by the fingers.

When two reins are involved, as with a pelham bit or a full bridle, the snaffle rein is always kept on the outside, running either under the little finger or between the ring finger and the little finger, as you prefer, and with the curb rein a finger's breadth to the inside. I prefer to let the free end of the rein drop straight down from the hand and rest on the near shoulder; but some good riders flip it over the near rein(s) instead. (Personally, I find this awkward, although it has the advantage of shortening the bight of the rein so that you cannot put your foot through it when you take a short hold and are riding short. I usually solve that problem by ordering shorter (cob size) reins, unless the horse has a vast expanse of "front.")

In order to take the reins in one hand or to stabilize the hands, you have to make a "bridge" by catching the right rein between the thumb and index finger of the left hand, placing it on top of the left rein and holding both together between the left thumb and index finger. The right hand can then be replaced on the right rein at whatever spot you wish. Most rein shortening is thus accomplished by first making a bridge with the right rein and moving the right hand closer to the bit, then repeating the action with the left hand. This method of rein shortening has the advantage of never losing contact with the horse's mouth and permitting rein adjustments, even major ones, to be made easily and quickly.

There is another method, useful when only small adjustments are required and you don't want to pick up a bridge: simply "walking" or inching your fingers up the rein. To do this, you permit a tiny bit of slack in your rein contact, then slide your thumb and forefinger a couple of inches up the rein to the point at which it passes between the thumb and the little finger; you then reset the thumb and forefinger while releasing pressure from the ring finger and little finger, and repeat as necessary. These procedures sound ridiculously complicated when described in writing, but they take only a second to perform, and all riders should practice them until they have become practically second nature.

Adjusting Stirrup Leather Length

There is a correct length of stirrup leather for every riding activity, and you'd think it would be an easy matter to find it. But I've observed that about half of all riders, even at the Olympic level, use the wrong length of stirrup over fences—usually too long. It's very hard to help a horse or stay out of its way if you can't get off your fanny; yet many riders somehow manage to convince themselves that they "can't ride" any shorter, even though they practically have to throw themselves at the horse to keep up with it in the air. I've persuaded a lot of riders (including some very famous ones) to pull their irons up a hole or two, and none of them has ever moved them back down. (My most dramatic conversion was a full four holes; and the convert was so thoroughly "born again" that he went out and won the Grand Prix of Aachen that very afternoon!)

What is the best length for you? Well, you can afford to ride pretty long for ordinary work on the flat or for elementary dressage, with the tread of the stirrup level with a point just below the ankle bone when your legs are fully extended. Some serious dressage riders ride even longer, but to my eye they seem to be fishing for their stirrups much of the time. For ordinary hunter riding and jumping small fences, I come up a hole or two, so that the stirrup tread falls somewhere between the middle and the top of my ankle bone. For bigger fences, I come up yet another hole or two; and for puissance fences, one or two on top of that, because there's nothing worse than a feeling of insecurity on a horse who's making the maximum effort that very big fences require. Fast work over steeplechase fences requires as short a leather as you will ever need (unless you go in for flat racing), and this would be something like eight holes shorter than your "normal" length.

There is a right way and a wrong way to adjust stirrups, and since any good rider has to do a lot of it, you should know the difference. The wrong way is to drop both reins and the stirrup, and then to look down and fumble around. The right way is to leave your foot in the stirrup iron, grasp the tongue of the stirrup leather in one hand (with the other hand continuing to hold the reins) and simply slide the buckle up or down on the tongue until it's where you want it, at which point you push the tongue of the buckle into the proper hole. Incidentally, it's a good idea to remove both leathers from time to time to see how the holes line up. If one leather starts to stretch more than the other, you can often equalize them again by placing the shorter leather on the near side, where it will be stretched as you mount from the ground. (If you are short and always get a leg up, you can accomplish the same thing by hanging the leather overnight with some sort of heavy weight attached to it.)

Tightening Girths

If you adjust stirrups in the right way, you never relinquish control over the horse, and the same thing should apply to your girth tightening. Leave your foot in the stirrup, and swing your left leg forward until it clears the saddle flap and knee roll; then grasp the girth billet with your left hand and make your adjustment. If the horse should do something in the interim, it is a simple matter to put your leg back in place and pick up the rein again with your left hand, so you remain in control. Note that the tradition is to set the girth on the off (right) side so that you have the right range for adjustment on the near side. If this is not the case, change it; and if you can't change it enough, for heaven's sake, get a girth that fits! Nothing is more dangerous (or more stupid) than a saddle that turns because it misses, by a hole or two, being able to be tightened sufficiently.

Riding Without Stirrups and Riding Bareback

The great advantage of riding without stirrups (if on the longe, without reins either), or of riding bareback, is that you simply don't have the leverage to do many things that are artificial and forced and therefore really wrong. At the same time, doing the wrong things that you *can* do both tires and hurts you. This is fine, because pain is a great teacher; it provides one of the strongest motivations to seek a better way. (Don't let anyone try to convince you that the "easy" way must be wrong. The fact is that the easiest, most economical way is always right, and should not be confused with the lazy way.)

It's not always possible to find a good longeing horse and someone at the other end of the longe line who knows what he's doing, but I urge you to seize every opportunity that comes your way. Otherwise, removing the stirrups (which I much prefer to simply crossing them over the pommel) and riding without any saddle at all are very beneficial exercises that you can do whenever you feel like it. Even dropping your stirrups and doing a turn or two of the ring at a posting trot is better than nothing. My very first riding instructor was a great believer in bareback riding, so I did a lot of it and showed in many bareback jumping classes as a kid. (They were a feature of most horse shows those days, when some shows even offered bareback equitation classes.) I must have benefited greatly from it, because my later teachers thought I had some riding talent, and I honestly don't believe I started out with much.

Doing It with Mirrors

Most indoor riding rings these days have some sort of mirror for you to use in checking what you and your horse are doing, and I encourage you to make use of them. It is surprising that many things that *feel* quite extreme are hardly visible in the mirror, and the converse is also true. Verify the feel with what it looks like in the mirror, and if the horse also signifies its approval by accepting what you're doing, write it all down in the notebook every rider should keep. Your notes will be no guarantee that you can reproduce the whole thing the next time, but they will at least keep you from wondering what your thoughts were when you thought you had invented the wheel, and in time and in aggregate they may lead you much closer to the truth than you were when you started.

Four

THE AIDS
AND THEIR
APPLICATION

*I*f riding is basically a matter of communication between a horse and rider, one might regard the aids as the vocabulary of the rider's body language. (I have long regarded the archaic terms "helps and corrections" as more precise than "aids," but let's stick to modern usage.)

There are two different kinds of aids that the rider can use in controlling the movement of the horse: natural and artificial. Five aids are usually considered to be natural (the hands, leg, back, weight and voice), while two more (the whip and spur) are artificial. Generally speaking, the aids can be used actively (when they are eliciting

33

a response), passively (when they are merely supporting or sustaining) or not at all. Their absence or removal may sometimes be interpreted by the horse as a reward.

The rider must have enough control of the aids to be able to employ them judiciously, on a graduated scale from 0 to 100. This requires them to be completely independent of the business of staying on! Let's consider them in turn:

The Hands

The rider's hands can do so much good and so much harm in so many different ways that there's a constant danger of using them excessively. The old axiom is as true as ever: the rider's hands are usually used too much, and his legs not enough. Nevertheless, hands are vitally important. You may have defects elsewhere in your riding technique and still be a good rider if you've got good hands; but you can't have bad hands and still be a good rider. After all, the horse's tongue and lips are as sensitive as your own; just imagine how it would feel to have someone's hands connected to your own mouth by some metal and leather apparatus!

German equestrian literature and much German teaching suggest that the hands should do no more than hold the reins, and that you should influence the horse almost entirely through your legs. The French, on the other hand, describe a wide variety of different rein effects and attach great importance to them, while acknowledging the importance of always supporting and coordinating them with the actions of the legs. The contradiction may be more apparent than real, because the best German riders use their hands a lot, even though their basic methods tend to presuppose the German type of horse that has less natural impulsion (therefore requiring stronger leg actions) than the Anglo-Arab and Selle Français strains preferred by the French, or the Anglo-American Thoroughbred. Having learned a lot from studying both approaches, I do not consider them impossible to reconcile.

Good hands will be stable (rather than unsteady); interesting (rather than boring or stupid); refined (rather than crude or clumsy); and fair (rather than arbitrary or punitive). The principal functions of the hands, as I view it, are to sustain or support, with fingers half-closed and a light contact (no more than a pound or so of tension on the reins); to resist, with the fingers pressed firmly into the palm and the arms supported by the rider's body; to yield, by opening the fingers and/or advancing the hand or slipping the rein; to displace weight laterally, through the action of the opening rein or the indirect rein; to displace weight from front to back, through the action of the half-halt; and to alert or warn the horse, or to break up muscular resistance, through the action of vibration. (When I "vibrate" the bit in the horse's mouth, I simply slip it from one side of the mouth to the other with my fingers and without adding any pressure at all. This is not to be confused with sawing on the horse's mouth with the hands and arms.)

The hands must be able to release the horse completely, holding the reins by the buckle; to resist the horse completely, the rider's fixed hand being supported by a braced back; and everything in between. Yielding with the hand is simple: you push your hands forward and/or open your fingers until only the weight of the rein is felt by the horse's mouth. Resisting is more critical, for if your hand and arm positions are false, or you do not know how to support your hand with a braced back, you cannot resist, you can only pull. (And as we have already noted, a pulling contest against a horse is lost before you start.)

To resist, you must first act with your back, and then close your fingers, pressing them into your palm "as if to squeeze a drop of water from a damp sponge," as it is often described. I prefer the image of squeezing a hard rubber ball, but in any case, the action is a very positive one, and while you don't want hands of stone, if there is too much "give" in your fingers why should the horse submit? If you can truly fix or immobilize the hand, supported by the back, you can quickly use less contact and get results; but if you cannot, every horse will finally try to force your hand.

What if you close your fingers and nothing happens? The chances are that there was insufficient contact with the horse's mouth, which means that you should shorten the reins and try again. But if the reins were correctly adjusted to begin with, you can accentuate the action of the fixed hand by slightly rotating the hands inward around the thumbs, so that your little fingers approach your body more closely and your palm faces upward toward your shoulders. (This action is clearly impossible for a flat-handed rider whose palms were facing the horse's shoulders, rather than his own stomach, to begin with.) If the action is supported by a braced back, it puts you in the strongest possible position to resist without pulling, and all the while you're able to release it instantly to the exact degree you wish.

An opposite effect comes from intentionally separating your hands more widely while flattening one or both. This action invites the horse to move into the "corridor" the hands have created, and is a very useful means (especially with Thoroughbred horses) of letting the horse pick up the tempo without your having to drive at it at all. Coming off a turn when jumping against the clock or starting down the diagonal at an extended trot while working on the flat are two appropriate instances for just this sort of action, and many riders habitually flatten their hands a bit as horses leave the ground if everything is in order and they need only to encourage.

I cannot stress too much the vital importance of restoring all aids to their normal state as soon as the horse has complied with them. Once the horse has gone forward, ease up on your driving aids; once it has shortened, open your fingers again enough to reward. It is very common to see exactly the opposite: the rider gets the horse to come back once, but never releases his closed fingers again, and spends the rest of the hour hanging in the horse's mouth; or, having gotten the horse to go forward, spends the rest of the day with his legs stuck halfway through the horse. The reason you want your aids to be effective is so that you can teach the horse to respond to them more and more sensitively—and so that you can use them less and less. (The old expression "crude but effective" is thus a contradiction in terms as applied to riding; means that are *truly* effective are also economical, and economy is essentially attractive and never crude.)

How about raising the hands? On occasion it is important to follow the horse's head upward as far as it wants to go, to prove to the horse that there will be no evasion of the bit permitted above the rider's hand. (One often reads and hears that high hands make a high head, but this is nonsense; high hands make a low head, and vice versa. Forced low hands invite the horse to live with impunity always above the bit.)

It is obviously critical that you soften the hand the instant that the horse responds to its action as a reward. Remember, too, that the use of the fixed hand is by no means restricted to a simultaneous death grip on both reins; the closing of the fingers can be intermittent or sustained, executed by only one hand or both and to any degree. Feeling a slight "pulse" of contraction in the fingers in synchrony with the horse's gait can help you to cadence, stabilize or collect the trot and canter, the pulsation in your fingers being supported by a soft pulsation of your calves.

When only one hand is active, the opposite hand still normally plays a supporting role. Usually the inside hand positions the horse and initiates its bending, but it is the outside hand that must predominate in controlling speed, impulsion and direction, if you are to be able to ride the horse from the inside leg to the outside hand.

Let me emphasize again how essential a correct position of the hands, arms and shoulders is to the correct functioning of the hands. There can be no effective resistance if the hands are flat and the rider's elbows cannot find support against his sides. Nor can there be light, elastic contact with the horse's mouth if the rider's elbow joints are locked in a position from which they cannot freely open and close. Flat hands that are forced low doom the rider to mediocrity, even though some teachers and even judges may consider them acceptable.

Finally, let me remind you that pulling or making a traction on the horse's mouth is never a function of the hand, nor is any form of punishment. If the horse does not respond to your closed fingers, simply shorten the reins and do it again. If you need to raise or separate your hands to make them active, move to the new position with soft contact, and only close your fingers when you get there. Punishing the mouth with the hands is *always* counterproductive, appealing though it sometimes seems when the horse appears determined to goad you into doing it. Your goal is that the horse learn to trust and enjoy your hand, and it can never do so if it expects to be snatched or jerked arbitrarily. Horses that live in fear of the pain your hand can inflict on their mouth will protect themselves as best they can, and the means they employ are all inimical to their best performance.

Leg Aids

The calf aid is brought into action by lightly supporting or stretching the back and then slightly flexing the calf and raising the heel. A stronger effect can be achieved by first dropping the heel and slightly turning out the toe, then very actively flexing the calf. This, too, should be supported from the back. (For that matter, the leg and back aids *always* work best in partnership; bracing the back automatically tends to involve the legs, and vice versa.) And then, of course, the instant the horse responds, everything must return to normal!

The progression of escalating leg aids goes like this: light added calf pressure; stronger added calf pressure; touch with the heel; touch with the spur; hard pinch with the spur. If nothing is happening at this point, reinforce the leg with the whip. (If you start to try kicking with the whole leg, the security of your own position will be in jeopardy and you may end up on the ground.) Note that the leg does not normally move *back* to become active, except when it is being used as a lateral aid of some kind. In fact, if anything, the opposite should be true, for the farther back the leg goes, the weaker its position. Sometimes, when you really need a very strong leg in an emergency, it's a good idea to reach back softly with both legs and then bring them very vigorously forward, thus finishing in a strong position instead of a weak one.

Many riders, especially in dressage, get into the habit of constantly tapping with their legs or spurs, believing that they're doing the horse a favor by supporting its forward movement. What they are really doing, however, is telling it: "Ignore my leg—it will go on tapping, no matter what you do, so you may as well pretend it isn't there."

The Back

The back is the most difficult and even controversial aid to try to pin down, yet it is also the most critical one, and can exert a decisive influence on the other natural aids in both positive and negative ways. The key to the correct action of the back is variable elasticity, and the horse will tell you when the action is correct and when it is wrong. When it is correct, you are able to use less and less hand and leg until the horse seems to read your thoughts and respond to your back alone. When it is wrong, neither hand nor leg seems to have any real influence, and it takes a big effort to produce any response at all.

If we consider the back to be more or less straight when it's inactive, halfway between flexion and extension, what do we do to brace it or make it active? I've read and heard dozens of answers to this vital question, and must have tried them all. A common prescription is to tighten the muscles in the small of the back, or to push the belt buckle forward, but many riders who say they do this seem to end up hollow-backed. I prefer a recipe that seems more complicated: first I stretch up slightly, tightening my abdominal muscles as well as those that support the lower spine; then I push everything below the waist a bit forward, while drawing the shoulders and everything above the waist slightly back. It helps if the rider takes a deep breath before starting to use the back, for this by itself tends to make you sit taller and expands your chest while supporting the small of the back. The total effect is to stiffen your trunk somewhat, but to the degree that you choose, and in a way that can instantly be released, as it is essential to do to reward the horse for compliance with your request.

Exaggeration in the form of a punishing rigidity is of course the primary danger. Once a rider discovers that he can influence the horse with his back he often becomes so intoxicated with the effect that he insists on continually "coming through" with it, and forgets ever to reward the horse. This eventually teaches horses to defend themselves, and some learn this lesson all too well. Trying to reform a horse that has learned to stiffen its back as a defense against the rider's rigid seat and back can be a daunting task. And sad to say, many fine riders have ended their years with serious back problems that originated, I suspect, in trying to make too much of a good thing. Once you learn to use the back, try to refine your use of this wonderful aid by seeing how little of it you can get by with instead of how much, and encourage the horse to release its back by letting yours swing with it as often as you can.

Riders whose "normal" posture on horseback is already hollow-backed may benefit from finding out what a straight back actually feels like, which can readily be achieved by backing up to a wall and applying the entire spinal column to it. Such riders often benefit from consciously straightening their backs (which may feel like rounding to them) before bracing them, which avoids the painful and ugly rigidity of hyperextension. What you want is a back that is elastically supported rather than rigidly braced, and it is easier to accomplish this if you start from a truly neutral, median position.

Weight

The great advantage of weight as an aid is that it never gets tired, can very powerfully enhance the action of the other bodily aids and yet can be used with infinite subtlety in every direction. I believe that every indication from the rider to the horse should normally be accompanied by a *slight* shift of weight in the appropriate direction. It sometimes helps merely to think of inclining your head in that direction, and everything else will follow. (It's reputed that some Spanish Riding School horses will do one-tempo flying changes in response to the slightest inclination of the rider's head to either side!)

The Whip and the Spur

Both artificial aids can be used either to give very precise and subtle indications to the horse, or (rarely, I hope) to administer punishment. The latter function can easily become counterproductive in terms of the former, because you want the horse to accept and trust your leg, and to have no reason to flinch from the whip. Since flinching from the whip is a lesser evil than mistrusting the leg, I generally prefer to see a horse that's doing something really wrong whacked by the rider's whip rather than abused by the rider's leg. (As you know by now, punishing the horse's mouth is so counterproductive that it should never be considered, even as a last resort.)

Incidentally, few sights are uglier than a horse with a bald spot or a callous under the spur—both obvious evidence that the rider's constantly tapping leg has taught his horse to ignore any but the most extreme leg aids. Remember, even a relatively sharp stimulus, if constant, eventually loses its effectiveness—if it doesn't first drive the horse mad!

The Voice

I consider the voice aid very important. I talk to my horses a lot, and let them know how I think they're doing. (Sometimes I even sing to them.) The tone of voice—whether sharp and annoyed, or calm and soothing—is a form of communication that they understand very well. If your horses are used to listening to you, you can use the voice to good effect in situations when you fear that anything else might rock the boat. For example, if you have a tight distance between two huge fences, you dare not risk steadying very much with the rein, but you can whisper, "steady" or "whoa" very gently, and get just the right result. (For this reason, I don't want my horses to slam on the brakes abruptly when I say "whoa"; however, I use the word a lot in ordinary riding, in varying degrees of intensity, so that the association is always there.)

Every rider should also have a "cluck" that works on every horse. When I give a loud cluck, I want my horses to move forward immediately. It's easy to train them to do this simply by clucking and hitting them with a stick at the same time until the desired response is there, and then refreshing their memory from time to time. The beauty of a cluck is that, like "whoa," it can be used in varying intensities, and without changing the other aids. A little cluck can often be enough to change the horse's mind when it's starting to think: "Maybe I should put in an extra stride here," or "I feel like stopping."

Along with some kind word or phrase (like "Good boy!"), a pat or two also provides a nice reward and a momentary break for a horse that is doing well or trying to do right. It only takes a second, and ought to be used much more often than it is.

I might add that there's a fashionable practice these days of giving the horse a straight-armed wallop, as if to knock it off its feet, when it has jumped a good clear round, or even worse, of making a swipe at its ears. These self-assertive displays of "kindness" seldom seem to be appreciated by the horse, and from the point of view of rational riding, you'll have to explain the whole thing to me.

Orchestrating Your Aids

All of your aids are capable of a wide range of effects and of being combined in an infinite variety of ways. Your skill as a rider will ultimately depend on your ability to coordinate and blend these different actions in a way that is coherent and comprehensible to the horse.

To use the most obvious example of this, your driving and retarding aids can be used not at all, or to the maximum of your physical ability, as well as everything in between. If you push the horse forward vigorously without the slightest restraint, you will have little control over its direction or rate of speed; if you use your restraining aids without any support, you invite the horse to drop abruptly behind the bit or to shift weight to the forehand so that it can more effectively resist. Thus in normal riding you always have to find a balance between the driving and restraining aids, both being present to a certain degree. You never make the hand active without supporting it with the back and leg; and you never make the leg active without modulating its effect with the hands (unless, of course, you are intentionally riding on a loose rein; and even then, the weight of the rein itself should provide the shadow of a "frame").

Influence

When all is said and done, you must remember that a sound position and correct application of the aids are not so much ends in themselves as means to an end—the end being to influence your horse, to get it to go where you want to go and do what you want to do.

Influence has many sources—physical, psychological and even moral—and good riders use them all. Riding shouldn't require a great deal of strength, but it does take some, as well as a certain amount of muscle tone and stamina. Sound mechanics do much to minimize the amount of sheer strength required, but a rider who cannot use his back and weight more or less correctly will never feel strong enough. Timing also has something to do with influence. Good riders seem to sense when they have a chance to "come through" with a horse, and they save their energy for those moments that can be physical and psychological turning points.

In the end, however, a rider who is timid about attempting to dominate the horse and is content to remain a passive "passenger" will remain one, no matter how correctly he rides, while a less skillful rider who's a real trier often succeeds by seasoning his efforts with a strong dash of determination.

Five

RIDING ON THE FLAT

Why is flat work important to the jumper? Because in large measure, the art of jumping is the art of riding good approaches: approaches that put the horse on the right spot, at the right speed and in the right physical and temperamental balance. Bad approaches make faults probable or even unavoidable; good approaches make good jumps practically the course of least resistance for the horse (at least within the limits of its ability). And approaches take place entirely on the flat. If a horse can't lengthen and shorten and turn obediently and in balance on the flat, how can you expect it to do so in its approach to the fence? (The only answer is a pretty

45

weak one: thanks to its instincts of self-preservation, without which we'd undoubtedly see even more jumping faults
than we do now.)

Flat work, then, is the principal end to which we put
the means of our position and our body language of aids.
Some riders may still harbor the delusion that the horse is
merely a vehicle to carry them when they "go riding." But
for the horse, riding is indistinguishable from training:
you're training your horse every time you ride it, like it or
not; and after every ride, your horse will have changed in
some way, for better or for worse.

In order to accomplish good work on the flat, that is,
in order to develop in the horse all the skills it needs to
execute perfect approaches and to condition its physical
mechanism in the most suitable way for its competitive
career, it will help a lot to understand the following basic
concepts:

First, *the horse is a rear-engined animal*. Just a glance
at the comparative size of the two ends should show you
that its real motive power is in the rear: the power to
push it forward, and to lift it (and you) off the ground in
jumping. The key to using this motive power most effectively is engagement: getting the horse to reach forward
with its hind legs well under its body. This rounds the
horse's back under the rider and "cocks" its entire musculature. You'll see some horses all "strung out," with
their necks inverted, their backs hollow and their hind
legs in the next county, and yet still able to make a jump of
some sort off their forehand. But their jumping style will
be very flat and lack a proper *bascule* or pivoting action,
without which they'll never be able to realize their full
potential.

Whatever you do on horseback, it is essential to keep
the engine turning over—to maintain the "revs," you might
say. And this means that what you do with your legs will
always be more important than what you do with your
hands. It's easy to overuse your hands and focus on what
the horse's head and neck are doing, because they're
right before your eyes. But you must never ignore what
the horse's hindquarters are doing, since the solution to
most of your problems lies back there. It's like sailing a

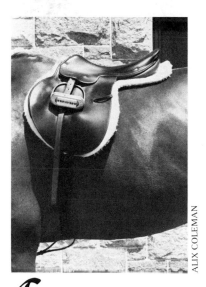

ALIX COLEMAN

ALIX COLEMAN

*A*t the left is my idea of a comfortable jumping saddle. Note that the deepest point is exactly halfway from pommel to cantle. At right, my preferred mounting method, with the rider standing at the horse's shoulder. Standing farther back makes you vulnerable to cow kicks.

PETER WINANTS

ALIX COLEMAN

*T*he wrong and the right way to adjust stirrups. Every good rider ought to be able to adjust stirrups blindfolded, using the method at right.

*A*t left, my idea of a normal leg position for general riding, the heel only slightly lower than the toe, with nothing forced. At right, a good length of stirrup leather for jumping bigger fences, a couple of holes shorter.

*A*t left, the "Old English" look, with the foot all the way "home" in the stirrup and pushed forward a bit. Not a bad position to adopt with a fresh horse or a horse that might buck or wheel, but not suitable for ordinary use. At right, an exaggerated leg, the heel forced too deep and the lower leg carried away from the horse's body.

*A*t left, a normal, general purpose seat. At right an exaggerated "forward" seat, everything too stiff (especially the back) and too forced.

*L*eft, a very deep seat with a long leg, suitable for elementary dressage training. At right, an unashamed "safety" seat, a useful position to adopt with roguish horses, dead green horses or in emergency situations.

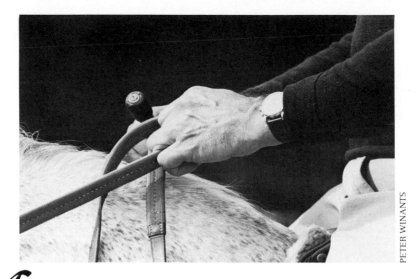

A normal hand position, the hands inclined some forty-five degrees from the vertical. I have never been comfortable with the rein going under my little finger.

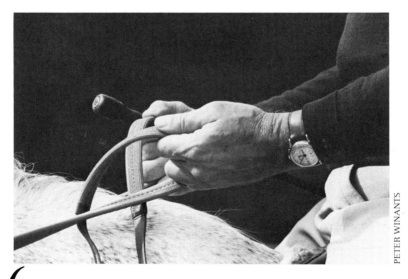

H ands in their most active position, slightly more than vertical (which pushes the rider's elbows into his sides). Note how the rein is fixed between the thumb and forefinger, as if by a set screw, leaving the fingers free to manipulate the reins.

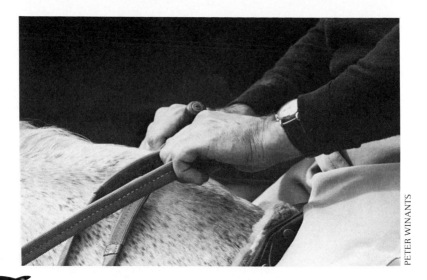

*F*lat hands forced low, the rider's palms facing the horse's shoulders, his elbows completely released from his own sides. Useful only if intentional passivity is desired.

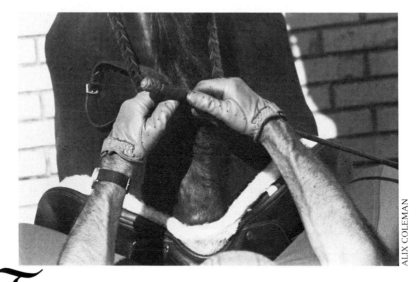

*T*he wrong way to hold a whip. Notice how the act of pinching the whip (along with the rein) between the thumb and forefinger tends to arch and stiffen the rider's right wrist.

*N*ormal hands, and the normal way of holding a whip, as seen from above.
Notice how the whip rests against the rider's upper leg.

*F*lat hands, as seen from above. Though many equitation judges accept this position I consider it a serious fault, especially because it tends to block the rider's hips from working inside his elbows so that they can support the hand from behind.

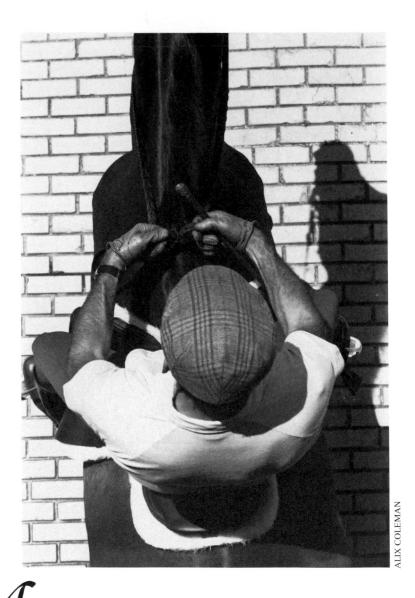

ALIX COLEMAN

*A*nother seriously defective position, what I think of as the "bear hug" attitude. The exaggerated arching of the rider's wrists tends to carry the elbows far from the rider's sides, so that they can find no support from his upper body; this means that he can never really fix his hand.

A normal position for the walk, the rider's back relatively straight, the line from his elbow to the horse's mouth also straight.

The posting trot. A very slight forward inclination and a very slight additional support in the small of the back make posting easier. The rider should feel that he is pivoting more on the lower calf than on the knee.

A weak position, the rider inclined too much forward so that he tends to get ahead of the horse.

A very strong position, with the rider's center of gravity well behind that of the horse. Too strong for normal use, but handy in emergencies.

ALIX COLEMAN

A good position for the sitting trot, the upper body vertical. (If it were inclined forward, the rider could only bounce.) Note the straight line from the rider's elbow to the horse's mouth; he is carrying his hands, and not resting them on the horse's mouth.

ALIX COLEMAN

A very common sitting trot position, with the rider's hands forced low, the straight line to the horse's mouth being broken underneath. I much prefer the position in the top picture.

ere's what the "bear hug" position of the upper arm looks like at the sitting trot. Note how it rounds the rider's shoulders.

itting to the extended trot. The rider must keep pushing his pelvis forward and resist letting his shoulders be drawn forward if he is to preserve a complete, no-bounce contact with the saddle.

ALIX COLEMAN

*T*oo much of a good thing: here the reins are too long, the hands a bit too high, the upper body a bit too far behind the vertical. A bit too "dressagy" for the jumper rider (but not quite correct for dressage, either).

ALIX COLEMAN

*P*osting to the extended trot. The hands are forced too low, but the balance of the upper body and its inclination are quite correct. The rider needs to push his pelvis forward as it returns to the saddle instead of letting it slip back if he wants to preserve the correct equilibrium of his upper body and his influence over the horse.

A correct position for the rider at the canter, the horse very much "in front of the rider's seat," the line from his elbow to the bit perfectly straight. I think it is important to really sit to the ordinary canter, which is not possible if there is much more forward inclination of the upper body than this.

This is what some riders laughingly call a canter in the show ring these days. With so much upper body inclination, there is no choice but to either roll or post to the canter, the buttocks leaving the saddle with every stride.

*F*or anything beyond a strong canter, the rider will usually prefer a half-seat. If he is sitting in balance, there should be no need to rest his hands on the horse's neck, but in either case, the half-seat should be clean, with no posting to the canter.

*I*n general, I prefer not to see the rider's upper body supported by his hands, whether on the flat or over fences, since it tends to create the illusion that you are "with" the horse even when you are ahead of its center of gravity.

ow I tie my stirrups up for longeing. The version at left is necessary if the stirrup leathers are fairly short, that at right even more secure if the leathers are a bit longer.

he preferred form of cavalletti, and the horse properly attired for longeing. In practice, I often make do without side or draw reins or proper cavalletti, and use rails on the ground instead. The longer here is Bertalan de Némethy, a past master, whose book on cavalletti and gymnastic work is indispensable.

boat: the tiller is useless if the boat isn't moving. Tempting as it may be to answer the horse's resistance with your hands, you'll usually find it far more effective to answer it with your legs.

Next, never forget that *the horse is bigger than you are,* and that it should carry you. It is not your job to try to hold it up, or to try to "lift" it off the ground in jumping! But because the horse is bigger than you are, neither should you ever get into a pulling contest with it, but simply resist instead, as explained in the last chapter. In fact, you must prevail over the horse using something like the techniques of judo ("the gentle way"), in that you induce the horse to place its strength at your disposal by dominating it through the displacement of its own weight.

In all of this, you must remember that the horse is your partner. Of course, there are all sorts of partnerships, some quite equal, others involving a considerable degree of domination by one of the partners. But it is important for the horse always to retain a sense of its own volition and spirit; if you dominate it to the point that it becomes only a prisoner, and cannot freely give itself to you, you will never get the best of which it is capable. In other words, if you can't get the horse to accept and enjoy its relationship with you, and to accept the mechanisms through which you communicate with it, then those measures aren't any good in the final analysis, no matter how effective they may seem for a while. I've seen a lot of horses that have been bullied by their riders and made to do everything through strength, coercion and the threat of pain. Their riders often brag about their accomplishments and all the things they can make their horses do. In the end, however, if the horse can't learn to like it, their riders' accomplishments are illusory and temporary, because the horse will always get the last word. Sometimes the word is funny, sometimes tragic (some riders aren't aware of what they've done until the horse "comes up empty," if then); but the horse will get that last word, even so.

Before we ask the horse really to concentrate and go to work on the flat, it's only fair to let it warm up a bit,

giving it a chance to get the kinks out if it's an older horse
or to get rid of some of its nonsense and playfulness if it's
a green horse or a young one. This can be accomplished
either on a longe line or on a loose rein at a brisk trot
and/or canter. Whichever you use, the purpose is simply
to get the horse's muscles supple and let it settle down
enough for serious work.

How should we begin our real work? Well, we know
that no horse can be pleasant to ride or obedient unless
we can compress it to some degree between our driving
and restraining aids—in other words, between our hands
and our legs and back—so that it is more or less "on the
bit" or "in a frame." This compression improves the engagement of its hind legs and thus somewhat rounds its
back under our seat (its antithesis being the hollow-backed
horse that goes with its head up in the air). So we start by
asking the horse if it remembers this engaged posture (or,
with a new horse or a fairly green one, if it understands it
at all).

In effect we are saying, "All right, now, let's be serious. Can you give me the sum of one and one?" I do this
either at the walk or the halt, and I accomplish it by
picking up the reins, adjusting their length and then closing my fingers on them while sitting a little deeper at the
same time, slightly supporting my back and closing my
calves very softly. In other words, I add a little drive but
do not permit the horse to express itself freely; instead, I
catch it with my fingers. If the horse answers, "Yes, of
course, one plus one is two," it will yield its jaw and
slightly flex at the poll. I then say, "Good boy!" by opening
my fingers and asking it to move forward (or more forward), while sustaining the new "frame" by only partly
closing my fingers. I find this an invaluable mechanism.

What if the horse is unable to come up with the right
answer, if it replies instead, "I haven't the faintest idea
what you want me to answer," or even, "Go to hell"?
Then you must intensify your request, patiently and gradually increasing the pressure of fingers and legs until you
have made it sufficiently uncomfortable for the horse to
want to seek relief. It may raise its head; if so, you simply
raise your hands and continue. It may offer to go back-

ward; you do not let it. It may wring its head; you continue to resist. Until finally, at some point in its random
evasions, it flexes its poll and yields its jaw. *Immediately*
you soften your fingers, relax your legs and pat the horse,
telling it through your body language, "Yes, that's what I
wanted; and that's the only response I'm willing to reward." Then you repeat the whole procedure.

This time you may get the desired response more
quickly; with a relatively green horse or a spoiled one,
maybe not. But within a few minutes, if your resistance is
effective and your rewards immediate, the horse will begin to get the idea: to soften its jaw and flex its poll the
minute you close your fingers and calves or slightly brace
your back. Now you can start to trot, or go ahead with
whatever other work you want to accomplish. But in my
experience, it's rarely useful to get out of a walk until the
horse can give you the right answer to "one plus one."

Some good horsemen will tell you that the above sequence is an unnecessary and dangerous shortcut, point-
ing out that if you have enough patience, and simply push
the horse forward into yielding hands, it will eventually
find its own balance and tell you that "one plus one is
two" without even being asked. You can then reward it
and proceed until it offers, again unsolicited, the answer
to two plus two. I must admit that this method works too,
and in fact can work very well. But it's not what I do—
perhaps because, as a weekend rider, I sometimes thought
I'd see the seasons change while I still waited for a response worthy of reward. In any case, I've only rarely
encountered a horse that *too* readily offered to come behind the bit in response to the method I've outlined, and
those cases were easily remedied by simply pushing the
horse forward more freely, and asking for a little less
frame.

I should mention a variant of the above mechanism
that can be very useful with badly spoiled mouths, and in
particular with high-headed horses that automatically in-
vert their necks in response to the pressure of your
fingers. With these, I suppose the first request should be,
"Say one." You do this by setting up a little resistance in
the fingers of only one hand (still supporting this action

from behind, of course), so that eventually the horse slightly yields its head and jaw to that side. You immediately say "yes" by opening the fingers on that side, and set up the resistance in your fingers on the other side. This mechanism has nothing in common with sawing on the mouth or attempting to force the head down. It is a process of alternate resistances and rewards on either side that can break up the resistance in the horse's neck and jaw and explain to it, through your body language, what you are asking for and what you are willing and eager to reward.

Once a foundation of compliance has been established at this very basic level, there are a number of related exercises that you can do at various gaits in order to further refine your communication with the horse. Again, they are best done first at the walk, then at the faster gaits only when the horse can consistently give you the correct "answers" at the walk.

(An obvious exception to using the above procedures is the "catch-riding" situation in which there is only minimal time in which to become acquainted with a strange horse. Then, instead of explaining, "this is how I ride," you discreetly inquire, "how do you like to go?" Whatever problems you encounter you simply ignore or finesse. Though it may be useful to know how to do this, it is hardly the preferred practice of good horsemen, which is why I dislike the present formula for the finals of the World Championship, with its exchange of horses.)

Four turns make a rectangle, but a continuous turn makes a circle. Turning (at the walk, to start with) offers a wonderful opportunity to explore and master a concept on which all German riders rightly place a good deal of emphasis: the concept of riding the horse from your inside leg onto the outside rein. This is not as easy as it sounds! (Bert de Némethy used to ask us to drop the inside rein altogether during turns to prove that we "had" the inside hind leg, and sometimes the turn would disappear along with the inside rein.) To get the right feeling, it helps to exaggerate a little at first, almost as if you were trying to do a shoulder-in on the circle.

The principal advantage in riding the horse on diagonal aids manifests itself not so much on turns as on straight lines, for it's much easier to make the horse straight if you still ride it from the inside leg to the outside rein, with almost a hint of "position" or bend. The feeling of having the horse on diagonal aids is obviously the exact opposite of the "handcuffed" feeling you get when the horse lugs equally on both of your hands and obliges you to hold up its head.

A very useful exercise in coordinating your aids and increasing the horse's attentiveness and responsiveness to them is one I learned from the famous Dutch dressage trainer Harry Gilhuys when he was stabled near me one winter. It consists of walking (and trotting) as slowly as possible without ever breaking into a halt (or walk), while still maintaining perfect continuity and smoothness of movement. It's hard to do well and is a good change of pace from the other exercises. (It reminds me of a famous bowing exercise for violinists: seeing how long you can sustain a single bow without breaking the thread of tone.)

An exercise that can be employed even in the smallest warm-up area is trying to make the horse run away with you at the walk, without ever breaking into a trot. It's really just another variation of the same basic idea: balancing the horse between hand and leg. Like the others, it teaches you one of the most useful things a rider can learn: how to drive and hold at the same time. In its extreme form, the same technique can be used to hold together tired horses who are jumping big fences at speed, which is why its principal application is in Three-Day Eventing and steeplechasing. But even in show jumping, if you simply drive a tiring horse toward the end of the course without supporting it, it will sprawl and flatten over the fences; while if you stop riding it from behind, it will start to plod and be unable to get to the far side of spread fences. By driving and holding at the same time, you can often prevent such catastrophes.

Though I don't like to leave a walk until the horse is more or less on the aids, I think that the trot is the most important gait of all for flat work and the essential foundation for everything else. With some horses, I've even felt that if you could produce the trot you wanted in the warm-up, you could jump a clear round in the ring without any other preparation. Of course, it has to be a really good trot—"keen but submissive," to use the FEI terminology —one in which you can place every foot just where you want it.

How do you develop such a trot? I wish it were merely a question of pressing the right button, but that has not been my experience. And only a handful of horses are born with it. The trot I have in mind is what was classically called "le trot souple"; and this "supple trot" is produced by making a variety of demands on the horse so that finally it simply prepares itself to comply with your next one, whatever it may be. It's quite different from the trot we use simply to loosen up a horse or get the kinks out, and it takes a lot of concentration from both the horse and rider. You obtain it by asking for more something— and when you get it, you ask for something else, then more of that. For example, you go forward, and then go forward some more, so that the horse gives itself up to you; you ask it to shorten, and then to shorten a lot; when it submits, you ask it to go forward again, or to give you a shoulder-in, or a few steps of a half-pass, or to halt. You keep the horse busy intellectually and physically until finally it balances itself and really puts its mind and body at your disposal. This is a marvelous feeling. You don't get it every time you try, but you should still look for it every time.

What we're talking about, of course, depends again (just as in the work at the walk) on balancing the horse between your driving and restraining aids, and alternating the dominant one. This needs to be done with great discretion, because it is important to avoid confusing the horse (especially if it is a young horse) when using your driving and restraining aids together. In fact, with a young horse, it's not a bad idea to revert from time to time to using the legs unopposed by the hands, and vice versa, in order to keep the essential distinction between them clear in the horse's mind.

Remember that the right moment to drive a horse at the posting trot is when your seat returns to the saddle. (It can't exert much influence while it's in the air!) If you're posting on the correct diagonal, this moment will occur when the horse's inside leg is on the ground (because the horse can't very well obey with a leg that's in the air either). Some people attach great importance to diagonals, and equitation riders are obliged to observe them scrupulously. (You're on the "correct" diagonal when you are rising as the horse's outside shoulder is moving forward.) I always ride young horses on the correct diagonal as part of the effort to develop them evenly in both directions; but if an older horse that has some aches and pains shows a preference for a particular diagonal, I generally acquiesce instead of demanding something that it finds uncomfortable.

Work at the Canter

The reason it's important to be very demanding about your trot work is because problems are so much easier to solve there than at a canter or gallop. The element of sheer speed, an intoxicating element to many horses, is present to a much lesser degree. But canter work is the essential gait for a jumper because when riding approaches to a fence, the rider must be able to play the stride like an accordion, extending and compressing it with fluency and at will, without upsetting anything else.

The strike-off into a canter is more than just an important detail, since it's much harder to retrieve something after a bad start than it is to preserve it correctly after a good one. A sloppy strike-off into a sloppy canter presents the rider with a problem before he gets anywhere near the fence, because he has to put the horse together in the canter before he does anything else, and time and distance may well run out on him before he gets it done.

The rolling canter depart from a trot is a perfectly acceptable alternative to the strike-off from a walk, provided that the rider brings the horse cleanly back into an organized canter instead of driving it forward into a sprawly one. The organized canter you want to start with is a slower gait than the extended trot; only the hand gallop is actually faster than the latter in miles per hour.

By simply drawing the horse's head to the wall while kicking with the outside leg, you'll produce some kind of a canter; but unless there is more support from the hands and your inside leg, and more straightness, it won't be the kind of canter from which you want to start an approach to the first fence of a jumper course.

Turns

The German word for a dressage arena is *viereck* (four corners), and you can't ride around a rectangular riding hall without making four turns. (Even an oval ring obliges the horse to turn twice during a full circuit.) So it's obvious that you can't go where you want to go in an enclosed space unless your horse turns well; and you certainly can't win any jumper competitions!

There are two basic ways in which the horse can turn. At collected or ordinary gaits in an oval ring or a dressage rectangle, it should *bend* around the turn (as the dressage riders say, "turn *through* the corner") so that its body actually conforms to the curve of the turn. In this kind of turn, the horse is bent around the rider's inside leg, its forehand held on the track of the turn by a slight inside leading rein and a strongly supporting outside rein. An easy way to put this sort of turn together is to "open the corner" by facing the new direction with your own shoulders. Your shoulders are thus parallel to the horse's, while your hips remain parallel to the horse's hips, resulting in a slight torsion of your waist with your weight very slightly drawn to the inside. The aids for the turn seem to function almost automatically when you open the corner with your body in this way.

The other sort of turn jumpers need is the one that's more appropriate at speed: when you're galloping, you have to lean into the turn in order to resist centrifugal force, just as a bicycle rider does, and permit the horse to turn on its inside shoulder, bending slightly opposite the curve of the track. (Even here, the horse must remain more or less straight; the shoulder should not bulge in as a defense.) Wide-radius turns are much easier to handle in this way. But every jumper should master both kinds of

turns in order to be able to use one or the other according
to the particular situation.

While we're talking about riding in a ring, let me add
that it's a good idea to adopt, *invariably,* the racetrack
practice of always riding past the gate or gap leading out
of the ring or to the barn, then circling back to it and
going straight out. Even (perhaps especially) horses that
aren't too bright always seem to know the way home. If
you always go past the exit before you circle back to it, or
use different exits if possible, your mounts will be much
less likely to think about ducking out as they approach
that end of the ring. At the racetrack, it is really dangerous if horses keep drifting toward the gap; in the show
ring, it can be enough to cause an avoidable resistance,
refusal or knockdown. So the best practice is never to let
your horses even start to think about it.

Basic Training Movements

This is not a book on dressage training, nor do I insist
that no jumper can perform well unless it has had a lot of
dressage training first. However, certain basic movements
of elementary dressage can be very helpful in developing
the horse's overall ridability and responsiveness to the
rider's aids, and mastering them with your horse will help
make your flat work more interesting, more varied and
more productive for both of you. You might think of these
skills as supplementary specialized tools that you can add
to your technical equipment. The larger your collection of
tools and the more deftly you can use them, the more
difficult the challenges you and your horse will be able to
cope with. Here I'll merely comment briefly on the basic
movements I have found to be most useful for a jumper. If
you'd like to experiment with them, I urge you also to
study a more comprehensive dressage text that discusses
them in the detail they deserve.

Transitions between the various gaits and transitions
of speed and impulsion within the gaits are invaluable for
the jumper, and I've discussed them earlier in less academic terms. ("Playing your horse's stride like an accordion" is essentially the same thing as making lots of

transitions, upward and downward.) The exercises described earlier that slightly compress the horse between your driving and restraining aids provide the basis for practicing transitions: when your driving aids predominate over your hands, the horse will lengthen and accelerate; while the predominant action of the hands will produce a downward transition and, if you continue it, eventually a halt.

All dressage movements, transitions included, will be facilitated if they are preceded by a slight gathering of the horse's forces and some signal that you are about to ask it to do something; and both of these functions can be accomplished by the **half-halt**. The term is rather misleading, since a half-halt should be more of an adjustment of the horse's equilibrium than a marked adjustment of speed. It is performed by doing several things more or less simultaneously: you stretch your torso upward and lightly stress the back by drawing the shoulders gently back while sitting deeper and pushing the pelvis forward by tightening the abdominal muscles, at the same time slightly closing the calves and closing the fingers. The hand may rise a little, and the forearm may rotate somewhat, bringing the little fingers closer to your body; but the hands must in no way be withdrawn, and there must be no traction on the horse's mouth.

If these aids for the half-halt are sustained and accentuated, the horse will come to a complete halt. Accurate, obedient, square halts are one of the hallmarks of a well-trained horse. Getting the horse to halt perfectly squarely on all four legs is not as easy as it sounds. I've found it helps to remember that the horse cannot stop squarely unless the last step is actually a *half* step; so you must catch the final footfall before it completes a stride of normal length, especially with the hind legs. But if you try to halt without supporting the action of the hand from behind, square halts will be mostly accidents.

Even though the horse has halted, it should still remain on the aids, able to move forward at your slightest indication. I think this condition ought to exist even when the horse is **backing,** which means that the horse should not drop out from under you and get stuck behind the bit.

In order to ask the horse to back, I bring my legs quite far back so that they create a sort of "chute" that will keep the horse straight as it moves backward, and then I make them gently active. Since the hands prevent the horse from expressing this stimulus in a forward direction, it steps backward.

It is important not to attempt to produce the backward movement with your hands alone; they should simply put the horse in reverse gear, so to speak, while the legs act as an accelerator to create the actual backward motion.

The **shoulder-in** is perhaps the most useful of all of the elementary dressage movements, because it develops the rider's influence over the horse's inside leg. And since we always want to ride the horse from our inside leg to our outside hand, exercises that strengthen this relationship are invaluable. In order to perform the shoulder-in, we bend the horse around our inside leg by bringing its shoulders inside the track, positioning them with the inside rein and holding them there by catching the outside shoulder with the outside rein. The outside leg prevents the haunches from swinging out. The horse is thus held on three tracks (its inside hind leg stepping in the same track as its outside front leg); it is curved and looking *away* from the direction in which it is moving. I like to alternate shoulder-ins and circles in which the horse moves in the direction in which it's looking.

Leg-yielding is a diagonal movement in which the horse moves away from the rider's leg and rein aids, laterally applied (on the same side), while the rider continues to support with the opposing leg and rein. The horse is slightly bent away from the direction of movement, somewhat as with the shoulder-in. Leg-yielding, like the other lateral training movements, is intended to make the horse more supple, obedient and responsive to the rider's aids, as well as to increase its engagement and collection.

Because it gives the horse a general idea of diagonal movement, I find leg-yielding a useful preliminary to the **half-pass,** in which the horse is bent the other way and is looking in the direction of movement, rather than away from it. It's hard to maintain amplitude and evenness of stride in the half-pass at a trot while maintaining the correct bending, as you must. It's important, too, for the rider's seat to remain in the middle of the horse, with his weight drawn only slightly in the direction of movement, without contorting his body or letting any part of it collapse. For a jumper, a perfect half-pass is an attractive but perhaps superfluous accomplishment, and I usually settle for just a few correct steps. But Three-Day horses have to learn to perform it very well, since the half-pass is an important element of their dressage test.

The only other basic dressage movement I use frequently is the **half-turn on the haunches** at the walk, because it is a good way of introducing some of the aid combinations required for the movements described above. When performed correctly, the half-turn on the haunches bends the horse slightly in the direction of the half-turn, and asks it to step around by means of the diagonal aids (inside leading rein supported by the outside rein and outside leg). The rider's weight is slightly to the inside. Many horses want to step out with the outside hind leg, or bend the wrong way, or pivot on the hind legs instead of stepping, or rush, or move backward, so this movement, too, is not so easy to perform correctly and precisely.

Circles and **figure-eights**, at both the trot and canter, have been a stock-in-trade of horse trainers at least as far back as 1550, when the first printed book on horsemanship (by Grisone) appeared. The figure-eight is really no more than two circles in different directions. Its main purpose is to prevent the horse from becoming one-sided, and to permit concentrated practice of the simple or flying change of lead at the canter. It is important, I believe, to start out by practicing the figure-eight as printed (in the form of two circles) rather than as handwritten (with a long diagonal connection). As the horse reaches the connecting point of the two circles, it should be momentarily straight.

The only exception I make to this rule is in approaching fences and then circling away from them (as described in detail in Chapter 6), for you then want to straighten out the line and hold the horse straight on the approach to the fence for several strides before you smoothly turn away.

Flying Changes of Lead at the Canter

There are innumerable ways of introducing the flying change, and I have tried a lot of them. Different horses find different things hard or easy, just as most horses seem to be born more or less one-sided. But whatever method you use, it's probably wise to start by changing from the lead the horse doesn't like so much to the one it prefers. (For ex-racehorses, this is likely to mean changing from the right lead to the left one.) Frankly, I've never had much success with one of the most frequently prescribed methods: making a simple change (that is, making a few walking or trotting steps before taking up the new lead), and then gradually shortening the number of strides between the two gaits until there are none at all. Clever horses seem to get the idea that the trotting stride is important, and they'll try to interpolate tiny ones even when there isn't time to do so.

I prefer to use a riding ring with square corners (a standard dressage ring is ideal) and to make a long turn on the diagonal from the approaching corner back to the one you've left, on the counter-canter. (More precisely, in dressage terms, you'd do collected canter H to K and counter-canter F to H, changing a few strides before you reach H.) In this way, the rail urges the horse to change, and then the corner almost insists. A slight touch with a dressage whip held in the outside hand also helps the horse to change and encourages it to jump into the change. The horse is being asked to move back to the lead it prefers, and that helps too. I don't introduce the opposite change until the horse is anticipating a change every time it returns to H (or F) on the counter-canter, and doing so cleanly and well. This method seems to me to work better for more horses than any other.

The principal danger in teaching lead changes is that the horse will change in front but not behind (becoming "disunited"), or else change late behind. Oddly enough, the disunited canter is a very stable gait, perhaps one of the most natural ones. At least, I've seen many zebra and wildebeest in Africa moving disunited, and that's the way almost every giraffe I spotted was moving. I like my jumpers to jump off the correct lead, but if they swap back on one end or both and if they're older horses who know their job, I rarely insist. After all, it's *they* that do the jumping, and if they have a preference for a particular lead over a particular piece of ground, I try not to distract them by insisting on the opposite one. Incidentally, you seldom see a horse make a fault as a result of a disunited approach, even though hunter judges will invariably mark you down for it.

Occasionally you'll come across an overly keen horse that uses one-tempo flying changes in place as a form of defense or an expression of anxiety. With such horses, it's counterproductive to practice a lot of flying changes, and far preferable to bring them back to a trot for changes of lead, except when actually on course. Fortunately, these cases are relatively rare.

Longeing

With longeing as with most activities, there's a right way and many wrong ways. The typical American longeing style is to put the haltered horse on the end of a rope, and then throw pebbles at it until it's worn down enough to ride. At the other end of the scale, such people as Bert de Némethy and Sylvia Stanier (who wrote a book about it) can work a horse on the longe line almost as effectively as they can under saddle, and impart a great deal of educational value along with the physical workout.

To do it right you have to have the right equipment, which consists simply of a decent longeing whip and a decent line. Many good horsemen would add a longeing cavesson, a surcingle and side reins; but I find it more convenient to longe the horse in its regular saddle and bridle, adding draw reins when necessary. The reins are knotted at an appropriate length and slipped under the stirrup leathers, which are tied up so that they cannot slip down. (The two best ways of accomplishing this are included in the illustrations in the first photo insert. Version 1 works fine for those who ride with a reasonably long stirrup leather; riders with a shorter leg will need Version 2.)

The first few times a young horse goes "on the line," it will be better off in a longeing cavesson or with the line simply snapped to the ring of the bit; and you should enlist an assistant to lead the horse on the circle to give it the idea of the whole thing. Later on, you can run the longe line through the near ring of the bit, over the poll and snap it onto the ring on the far side. Since this arrangement gives you quite a bit of control, it should be used with discretion until the horse has become accustomed to it.

Just as the prime precondition to normal riding is the horse's willingness to stretch the rein and offer to go forward, the key to longeing is the horse's willingness to keep slack out of the rein laterally and to stay on the circle. In other words, the horse must not be permitted to cut the circle whenever it feels like it (which is why it's essential for your longeing whip and its lash to have a reach of ten or twelve feet). To start, you hold the longe in the hand nearest the head in the direction of the horse's movement (usually the left hand if you're right-handed), and hold the whip in the other hand. Then you carefully back away from the horse, watching to make sure that it doesn't suddenly wheel and kick at you out of sheer high spirits. (Carelessness about this once cost me a broken arm.)

Ask the horse to walk on a small circle for a turn or two (unless it's very fresh and unwilling to do so, in which case it will pick a gait itself). You should place yourself so that you are turned about twenty degrees in the direction of its movement, with your body just even with its quarters and the whip pointed about at its tail. You are now in a good position to keep the horse between your hand (the longe) and your driving aids (the whip). Should the horse slow down and put you even with its head, you need only take a step backward in order to regain your original position opposite the point of its hip; then drive it forward again with a cluck or a touch of the whip. Should the horse attempt to cut the circle and put slack in the longe line, the remedy is the same.

Some longers make a point of anchoring themselves in one spot and swiveling on their heels, but this strikes me as plain lazy. The advantage in making a slight turn in the direction of the horse's head is that it brings the whip hand closer to the horse's quarters, while the hand and arm that hold the longe line cross your body at the waist, which can provide support for them if necessary. Thus positioned, the longer should make a small circle of his own, no more than a foot or two in diameter, always maintaining his position opposite the point of the horse's hip, with its body and forehand ahead of him.

Daily Work and Schooling

Every time you get on a horse, you should have a pretty clear idea of what you hope to accomplish before you get off an hour or so later. (What you can't accomplish in an hour probably ought to be held over for the next session, while what you can accomplish in only fifteen or twenty minutes usually isn't worth accomplishing, at least from the educational point of view.)

Some overachievers get into the habit of drilling their horses every day, with astounding results—for a while. I remember a famous Olympic dressage rider whose horse got better and better until it was virtually letter-perfect two weeks before the Games. On the big day, however, the brilliancy and reliability had vanished (along with about a hundred and fifty pounds of body weight) and the horse could do little more than go through the motions. As a general rule, you won't go far wrong if you settle for a steady improvement rate of 1 or 2 percent a day, even including the occasional day when everything goes wrong, or nowhere at all. Any horse that can improve at a rate of 100 percent a year is bound to achieve its full potential!

In planning daily work, remember that the average show horse's life is not unlike that of a prison convict. It is constantly confined, its exercise is supervised and involves fairly hard labor, its diet is imposed and aside from traveling to competitive venues and competing, it can lead a life of relentless monotony. Riders should be aware of this and do as much as they can to provide sufficient variety in the horse's daily work for it to maintain a fresh and cooperative outlook. You certainly don't want your horse to think to himself when you arrive for your riding session, "Oh, God, here he comes again."

Your daily work program will usually emphasize one or more of five different kinds of content, and will often include a bit of all of them: Conditioning (galloping), reviewing past lessons, learning something new, hacking and riding on a loose rein and schooling over fences.

One of the most important elements, as well as one of those most frequently neglected by jumper riders, is conditioning. Many talented horses "run out of gas" over long Grand Prix courses, and no wonder! You have only to look at them more closely to see that they have no aerobic fitness, because they never gallop. Galloping on a real track, on hills, or on a beach would be ideal, but even twelve or fifteen turns around a good-sized riding ring at a half-speed gallop will open up the lungs, and it's better than nothing. The rider should always take a look at the muscle tone of the horse's intercostal muscles (and his own too, for that matter) when appraising its condition. You can take weight off by cutting back on feed; but galloping is the only thing that really helps the wind.

The second ingredient of your daily work is reviewing what the horse already knows, and most of your riding with a "made" horse will consist of this alone. It will concentrate on variations in speed and collection at all gaits, including turns around various fixed points (jump standards, trees or whatever is handy). Everything that contributes to perfecting the horse's approaches on the flat comes under this heading, for the rider will need absolute control of speed, impulsion and line in order to cope with whatever problems next week's course designer may pull out of his sleeve.

Third comes work on new material: technical problems either on the flat or over fences, such as distance problems, combinations or gymnastics, flying changes of lead, lateral work, counter-canter and anything else the horse has not already mastered, more or less.

A fourth essential ingredient, too often neglected, is riding on a loose rein. The more concentrated its actual work is, the more often the horse should be permitted at least a few minutes to relax its muscles and its mental concentration. Occasionally walking halfway around the ring on a long rein with the neck stretched is enough of a reward in the course of an hour's work; but every ride should end with a nice walk of at least ten minutes or more during which breathing can return to normal before the horse is turned over to a groom for washing and proper cooling out. If the rider is his own groom, twenty minutes or more may be spent this way, since you'll want the horse to be fully cooled out (inside, too) before you return to the barn, unless you plan to give him a bath.

In addition to daily relaxation on a long rein, every horse will benefit from one day a week of just hacking out in the woods or across country, if possible. This is a wonderful antidote to all the concentrated ring work, and especially to showing. It's also a great way to keep the horse's mind and body fresh and willing.

Next on the work program comes "proper" schooling: schooling over courses or parts of courses. Older, "made" horses that are showing regularly need only school once a week or so between shows to "keep them going" and in the habit of jumping courses. Such courses should be of a comfortable height—four feet to four and a half feet. Only an occasional bigger fence should be enough even for open jumpers, because the rider's principal concern is to perfect the horse's jumping *technique*. It should be able to lengthen and shorten at will, turn perfectly and solve most problem distances in either of the two possible ways (with and without an extra stride), so that the rider will have a complete set of options available and in working condition when he gets to a show.

Finally, of course, every horse is entitled to one day a week of complete rest: a turnout, hand-walking and grazing or, if these are impracticable, twenty minutes on a longe line just to keep the blood circulating. Just as with people, a single day of rest a week can do much to restore physical and mental freshness, and make the working time that much more productive.

What you're really trying to accomplish with this sort of schedule is to build up or restore the horse's "credit balance" so that you'll have something to draw against in competition. I've often thought of it in just these terms: during a show, you have to ask the horse to do a lot of difficult things: to go fast, make sharp turns, jump big fences and trust you a lot, even though you may have to be rather rough and far from "classical" in doing what you think you have to do in order to win a class. You've probably used a lot of temporary expedients and made some compromises. Now, after the show, it's time to make some new deposits to cover all of those withdrawals. When horses suddenly begin to lose form and perform worse and worse, it usually means either that they are developing some physical problem, or that there have been too many withdrawals without putting enough back. The next check bounces. It's important to keep this in mind when planning a horse's competitive schedule, because a constant grind of showing—even a constant grind of schooling—will eventually and inevitably lead to diminishing returns and, if carried to the extreme, bankruptcy.

Six

RIDING
OVER
FENCES

What is a good jump? For the horse, it's a fence that is negotiated cleanly and smoothly in an arc appropriate to the plane of the fence, with a takeoff, flight and landing that are all in approximately the same equilibrium. The preconditions for this, as we have seen, involve arriving at a good take-off spot in the right stride, at the right speed, with the right impulsion and in the right physical and temperamental attitudes. Given these favorable preconditions, a good jump is practically the course of least resistance for the horse (presuming, of course, that it possesses the innate ability to cope with the fence in question), because refusing or

even making a poor jump would require even greater
effort. It follows that much of the art of jumping lies in
riding perfect approaches. If you can consistently put your
horse in the right spot with the right wherewithal, you're
going to jump a lot of clear rounds.

Assuming that the approach was good, what should
the rider do during the jump? My basic answer is, "almost
nothing." Most of the moves a rider can make to "help"
a horse over a fence are either hindrances or irrelevancies.
The best thing he can do is to sit perfectly still, fold up
smoothly and maintain everything he had when leaving
the ground (including contact with the horse's mouth)
throughout the flight and landing. Visualize for a moment
what it would feel like if you were asked to jump a fence
with a fifty-pound knapsack on your back. Would you
prefer to have it securely strapped to your back, right over
your center of gravity? Or would you like it to be moving
around as you jumped, "helping" you?

In my concept of an ideal jump, when the horse ar-
rives as described above, the rider is sitting right in the
middle of his horse, keeping it balanced between his hands
and legs. If the rider has been in a half-seat between the
fences, he very gently eases himself back into the saddle
two or three strides out, perhaps adding just a tiny bit of
pressure with his legs as an expression of confidence and
support to the horse. I think a full seat before takeoff is
essential for a show jumper, because it provides the best
two-way communication we have; if the horse is thinking
of stopping, for example, we're much quicker both to
sense it and to do something about it from a full seat. It's
impossible to feel or influence the horse through your
seat if it's up in the air.

As the horse takes off, we do *not* attempt to synchronize with it a little jump of our own, with the purpose of
pushing us off the rear of the cantle to a point just behind
the horse's ears. If we have been sitting where we be-
longed during the approach—in the middle of the horse
and in balance—the horse's jumping action will automatically fold us up in the air. We can then softly and slowly
unfold on landing, so that the path described by our two
centers of gravity remains in perfect harmony, and we

land in a perfect mutual balance, ready for whatever comes next.

Good jumpers make a strong move off the ground, jumping right *into you* (or so it feels). They can even make you fold up too much, if you don't resist enough. On the other hand, if you resist too much, leaving your knee and hip angles too open, you'll feel as if you're hanging up in the air like a big bird, miles above the horse's back.

Horses that jump with a hollow back ("splinter bellies," in current vernacular) don't fold you up much at all, and some equitation coaches actually prefer this kind of horse. Personally, I've always hated riding horses that jump only by folding their legs, since it's associated in my memory with the sound of falling timber.

Let me emphasize again that the horse jumps first, and we go with it, rather like absorbing a bump on a ski run. Thus, if the horse refuses, we're still sitting on its back where we can make an instant correction, instead of sitting on the ground and wondering where the horse has gone. Moreover, because we have our legs on the horse, and the same contact with its mouth that we had on leaving the ground, expert riders can subtly influence both the arc and direction of the jump in the air with their body language. For example, we can add a little leg and release a little contact, thus encouraging the horse to land deep and take a long stride on landing; or we can support it in the air and ask it to pitch in more steeply; and we can start or continue a turn as we leave the ground so that we are almost turned by the time we land, already on the quickest line to the next fence that may win us the class.

The worst things we can do are to disturb the horse's jumping effort through some violent body movement; suddenly to abandon all support in an exaggerated "release"; to hit the horse in the mouth, even accidentally; or to get left behind. All of these occurrences can result from efforts to *do* something in synchrony with the horse's jump, instead of simply eliciting the jump and then going with it.

What are some other common mistakes in jumping form that can cause disappointing or disastrous results? Many riders, after riding the approach in a half-seat, snap shut as the horse leaves the ground and push their hands up the crest of its neck, thus abandoning all contact and supporting their upper body with their hands. In the air they are ahead of the horse and ahead of their own base of support. During the descent, they snap open again, but they still have to reestablish contact with the horse's mouth during the first landing stride. What's so bad about that? To begin with, by "dropping" the horse on takeoff, they invite it either to refuse, or to pick up speed in the air, and they are incapable of shaping its arc in any way. By snapping open on landing, they risk a hind knockdown. Having no influence on the first landing stride, it's not until the second that they can do anything about turning or shortening, since they have to reestablish contact first; and because this must be done so hastily, it is often rough. This pattern is very common in equitation classes, and for all I know it may be necessary or even desirable with beginners. But I also know this: if they're taught this technique at the start, they've got to learn a better one later on in order to ride really well.

The other worst faults in jumping form involve those many riders who try to anticipate when the horse will jump so that they can *do* something themselves (usually make a little jump) at the same time. Riders who have ridden their approach sitting way back in the "rumble seat" *have* to do something in order to avoid being hopelessly "left behind"; and this is just what happens to them when they expect the horse to make one more stride before the takeoff and it doesn't do it. Even riders who are sitting acceptably may get into trouble if they fail to wait for the horse to jump. In their case, expecting the horse to leave, they make their mini-jump from the saddle only to find that the horse puts in another stride instead of taking off. And so they're often on the way down as the horse is on its way up, and its takeoff either shakes them loose from the saddle or propels them into outer space.

But what should you do if you know that, given the circumstances of the approach, the horse is certain to knock down the fence if you ride normally? Well, the good rider does something *else,* almost anything that is different from what he normally does. And this is one of the things that distinguishes a good rider from an average or poor one.

During ordinary schooling, you shouldn't take heroic measures to avoid a knockdown. Knockdowns are a part of the horse's education. In fact, it's not a bad idea to run through a fence from time to time with horses that aren't too bright to begin with, or are a bit lazy, or are happy to let you do all the thinking and never give a moment's thought to adjusting their stride or helping you to do it. It helps to turn their brains on, and it's easy to set up: just sit there, like a bad rider. Needless to add, you shouldn't overdo it. Don't arrange a situation in which the horse could make a really bad mistake and fall, over an oxer, for example. Pick a nice vertical and let your horse get fairly tight to it and hit it; this reminds it that it has to bring something to the party too. I do not consider this lying to your horse (a thing I'd never do); it simply tells the horse that it can't leave *everything* to you.

In competition, however, it wouldn't make sense just to sit there, knowing that if you don't intervene there will be a knockdown. If the horse's approach is going to take it too fast and too deep, you should sit against it throughout the takeoff and refuse to abandon the support you've been giving it by making a release. Make the horse jump against your hand as much as you dare. In the opposite case, when you're late to a spread fence and will really have to reach for it, don't insist on sitting in the middle of the horse, but get up behind its ears if you think it will help it to clear the fence.

In schooling, you work as hard as you can to be classical and to develop a strong technique. But in competition, you must let your instincts and experience take over, and do what you feel you have to do. Good riders never give up. They fight to jump fences cleanly just as long as they think their influence can help the horse to make a better jump. If they have to do something "wrong" to produce a clean round, they do it. But they try to figure out what went awry and correct the underlying cause during the next schooling session.

Another thing good riders do only in competition is

to "call on" the horse to make a special effort, or to be extra careful in jumping a particular fence (usually the "bogey" fence on the course, often a big vertical that comes down very easily). Some riders bump the horse in its mouth, or attempt to lift it off the ground with their hands; but I find this very risky and often counterproductive, since it's easy to overdo it. More effective, I believe, is a *late* release in which you seem to restrict (through pressure alone, not a nick or a jab) the horse's takeoff. When the horse feels it has got to make a special effort because of that restriction, you go with it and let it explode. This is not a beginner's technique. But you'll see the best riders using it quite often when the chips are down, and it has more than a little to do with their success.

Another special situation is the dangerous one when the horse makes a bad approach to the kind of fence that could tip it upside down. In this case, a good rider doesn't hesitate to "cock his toe," sticking his feet on the dashboard and leaning back with his body, in hopes of riding out the storm or, if the worst happens, being in a better position to bail out. I hope you won't find yourself in this situation very often. But whenever you think your horse is headed for disaster, it's not a time simply to sit there, trying to look pretty. Every rider needs a dependable survival tactic in the form of an effective "safety" seat.

At the opposite extreme of a "safety" seat is the arc you need for the situation in which the horse is late getting to a big spread fence and needs all the help you can give it to reach the other side. This is one instance in which it is *not* advisable to sit in the middle of the horse, just as your instincts tell you. Instead, you should get as far forward as possible during the takeoff, and hold yourself there by refusing to close the angle in your knee. At the same time, you should deliberately abandon contact with the horse's mouth, feeding it so much rein that you cannot possibly retard its flight through your hands. If you do all these things, you'll have given your horse every chance to extricate itself from the bad situation. You won't look very pretty if a photographer happens to take your picture going over that fence, but there's a good chance that you'll leave the fence intact.

Obviously, there are many intermediate stages between the defensive seat and the extra-forward one, just as on the flat; and you should use them in their more moderate forms appropriate to the circumstances as you judge them. Being able to sit just slightly against a horse or to loose-rein it a bit as the situation demands are skills that enlarge your store of technical resources. Good riders over fences never remain frozen in a single position any more than do good riders on the flat. They move freely among whatever positions are most appropriate to what the horse is doing, as their feelings dictate.

Falls and Falling Off

Novice riders often brag about never having fallen off, in the mistaken belief that it makes them sound more expert, when in fact it only brands them as novices. If you ride enough to become proficient, you're bound to fall off; and if you ride over difficult courses, a certain number of falls is inevitable. I must add this, however: if you refuse to anticipate and "drop" your horse as it leaves the ground, you should not fall off very often; and if you ride sound approaches, you shouldn't have many falls. I've heard a lot about horses "never leaving the ground," but most of those I've witnessed had no choice: their last approaching stride put their chest right up against the jump. This situation leads to the very worst type of fall. As a general rule, you'd do better to "go for it"—to try to leave out the half-stride in an impossible situation—rather than to ride the horse right to the base of the fence. With the first way, you may get off with only a bad knockdown; but you're likely to end up on the ground or even in the hospital with the second. (I should add that chickenhearted horses won't be brave enough to leave out the half-stride when you ask them to, which is one more reason for avoiding them like the plague.)

I'm not sure that I can tell you *how* to fall, for I'm not sure I know myself—at least, not the way that tumblers and gymnasts know how to fall. But I do know that there comes a point with a falling horse at which you'd better bail out and stop trying to stay with it. For me, this involves a conscious though instantaneous decision and the thought "here goes nothing," as I let myself be thrown. The feeling is almost one of relaxing and accepting the inevitable, then tucking in your head and rolling away from the horse when you land.

Merely falling *off* is a less complicated matter; you can even sometimes manage to land on your feet. (But try to avoid the horse's feet as you do so!) Even if you land on some other part of your body, the worst bruise will probably be to your ego, which is as it should be. Chances are that you were doing something wrong enough to have deserved the fall, and you should spend some time thinking about the mishap and about what you can do to avoid a repetition of it.

Seven

TRAINING
THE
JUMPER

Although nobody expects a child to solve algebra problems without having learned arithmetic, some riders persist in trying to win hunter or jumper competitions with horses that clearly cannot negotiate a simple, single fence without revealing a weak or nonexistent elementary foundation for jumping. This is both sad and unnecessary, for giving the horse good enough fundamentals for it to realize its full potential (or at least most of it) isn't all that complicated or time-consuming. Nor does it require extraordinary riding talent. As in teaching any other skill, it depends mostly on using a method that is rational and progressive.

I'd started lots of jumpers, using a variety of methods, long before I was introduced to the basic elements of the system I now use by Captain Bertalan de Némethy, the distinguished coach of the U.S. Equestrian Team for a quarter-century. After seeing what Bert could accomplish his way, I have never relied on any other basic method, though I've added some variations here and there. The result is a procedure that is seamlessly progressive and virtually foolproof.

We must assume as a precondition that the prospective jumper has already mastered the ABCs of stop, go and turn at all three gaits, as outlined in the previous chapter. But as soon as the horse's basic skills on the flat are well underway, we can start to build its foundation as a jumper, starting with a fence reduced to its simplest terms: a single rail on the ground, or cavalletto.

Strictly speaking, a distinction should be made between rails placed on the ground ("trotting poles" to the English) and proper cavalletti, which are supported in some way to elevate them a few inches or more above the ground. (The Italian word *cavalletto—cavalletti* in the plural—means "little horse"—or "little horses"—and refers to what we call a sawhorse, something that elevates materials for the carpenter.)

Cavalletti are most practical to work with if they are solid, stable and not easily displaced. The ones we had at Gladstone were made of logs with feet that were notched as in log cabin construction, and they were perfect. They were also expensive to make, however, and suitable for no other purpose. So in practice, many of us make do with ordinary rails on the ground, using a little dirt pushed against them to keep them from rolling. These are more versatile, and less stressing to the hocks than the higher structure of proper cavalletti. (I've sometimes suspected that the latter might tend to aggravate incipient hock problems, and no horse needs that!) Since I'll be using the two terms interchangeably, you should know that if you've got a good set of proper cavalletti, you can use them whenever I refer to rails on the ground, and vice versa.

The great thing about using cavalletti and rails on the

ground is that they enable you to isolate and expose, in their simplest form, many of the problems and weaknesses horses will demonstrate over bigger fences. For example, most horses that raise their heads during the last stride or two of an approach to a fence and want to hurry will do exactly the same thing when trotting or cantering over a single rail on the ground. And any horse can quickly be taught to walk over the rail without making this mistake, then trot over it and finally canter. When it will canter over the rail on the ground without doing anything wrong, it will usually also trot or canter over little verticals and oxers correctly, and eventually over bigger fences too.

Now that the preliminaries are out of the way, let me explain the whole procedure, step by step.

You begin by circling, at a walk, over a single rail on the ground, keeping the horse perfectly on the aids. You want it to step cleanly over the rail, without hurrying, stumbling, slowing down and especially without raising its head. With a green horse, you'll rarely need more than ten or twelve repetitions before it starts to negotiate the single rail confidently and well; but with a spoiled horse or an inveterate "rusher," it may take many times that number. Whatever it requires, there's no point in going further until this simplest of all exercises is negotiated perfectly.

Once the horse is circling correctly in one direction, go the other way. When the horse is walking over the single rail perfectly in both directions, you can try the same thing at the posting trot, using the same criteria. Many horses will be tempted to jump over the rail at this point, but you should discourage this by raising your hands slightly, and/or by adding a little pressure with the fingers or vibrating the bit in the horse's mouth as you approach the rail. You may wish to revert to walking over the rail a couple of times. If the horse has had a decent education on the flat, it should take no more than fifteen or twenty minutes before it is trotting over the single rail correctly most of the time.

In remaking spoiled horses, you may wish to remain

at this point for several days, until the horse only very rarely makes a mistake, before adding a second rail. But more often, both steps can be taken in the first half-hour. The second rail should be placed parallel to the first, at a convenient distance for the horse's stride at a controlled working trot. Four feet nine inches to five feet is the average distance, but you should set it precisely so that the horse is not obliged to shorten or lengthen its stride at all in the beginning. At first, many horses will be tempted to jump over the pair of rails, and it may take some patience to explain, through your fingers, that you wish it to step over them. But the average green horse can usually learn this in the first lesson.

Jumping at Angles

Since the show jumper (as well as the equitation horse) will be asked to jump fences at angles throughout its competitive life, I think it's useful to introduce this from the very start and to incorporate it in the training program of horses of every level. As soon as the horse is stepping over the rail on the ground perfectly when approaching it at right angles, you may walk across it at a slight angle to the left, for example, then at a slight angle to the right. From then on, whether at a trot or canter, and over any kind of fence from a single rail on the ground on up, I occasionally vary the normal straight approach by angling it and/or by turning immediately after the obstacle. A horse with this experience at an early stage will never be taken by surprise when asked to jump from an angle, because it has learned to be prepared to cope with anything at which it is pointed, whatever the angle, from the very beginning.

Trotting over a single rail is the first note in the show jumper's scale; and just as musicians practice scales their entire life, so will the show jumper trot over rails on the ground forever. It's an indispensable reinforcement of the basics that everything else depends upon.

When the horse is trotting over two rails confidently and correctly, the next step is to add a third rail, then a fourth and a fifth. These additional rails should cause no

*I*n a perfect jump, the rider should feel that he does nothing at all in the way of jumping or trying to "lift" the horse off the ground when the horse jumps. He should simply sit in the middle of the horse and let the horse fold him up, while trying to maintain the same contact with the horse's mouth in the air that he had leaving the ground. That's what these two jumps with Sinjon (above) and Riviera Wonder (below) felt like to me.

*L*eaving the ground over a small oxer (above), the rider simply waits for the horse to jump. If his body has had the right forward inclination during the approach, he will open up as the horse rears off the ground (below)...

*A*nd then fold up again in the air. The hands simply follow the horse's mouth, letting the opening and closing of the elbows permit this to happen; during the descent (below) the rider maintains his forward inclination, instead of snapping open immediately, and remains in a position to influence even the first landing stride, if necessary.

*J*umping bigger fences is exactly the same, except that there must be a
stronger dynamic to the approach and the jump; the rider must permit
the horse to achieve a sufficient balance between pace and impulsion to
be able to jump the fence.

*T*hen he simply goes with the jump and lets it happen to him unless there is some special reason to start turning as he leaves the ground, or to influence the trajectory of the horse's jump in some way or other. For in general, nothing you can do "helps" the horse more than sitting still.

*H*ere is what I mean by trying to achieve a continuity of everything through an entire triple-combination. In particular, I want you to look at my hands and their contact with the horse's mouth, and where my center of gravity is in relation to the horse's throughout the sequence.

*A*s you can see, there is no reason to abandon control over the horse at any point, and if you don't "drop" the horse as it leaves the ground, there will be no need to reestablish contact and control after you land. This is especially important if you need to adjust the stride between fences.

PETER WINANTS

*T*he position above is a very vulnerable, "sitting duck" position, the rider having left the ground ahead of the horse with a stiff, hollow back. Only the hands are correct; everything else seems exaggerated, but in a way that equitation judges—regrettably—often seem to like.

L'ANNÉE HIPPIQUE

I'm not quite sure why I was in such a strong defensive position over this relatively little fence at Hickstead, England, but this is how you ought to sit on a horse that wants to get strong when you don't want to let him gain an inch on you. The feeling is a bit one of letting the horse jump away from you instead of going right with him, and it's a useful move to have in your repertory.

The ideal form of cavalletti, not too high, but heavy and very stable. With a double set like this, you can use slightly different spacing on each to accommodate different lengths of stride.

In the absence of specially constructed cavalletti, however, a rail on the ground works almost as well. The single rail really represents a fence, reduced to its very simplest terms. Until the horse will negotiate this perfectly, first at a walk and then at a trot, its basic foundation as a jumper will be flawed.

*T*he next step in the sequence of jumper training is to ask the horse to negotiate two rails, spaced about four and a half feet apart, with the same perfect equanimity, without altering its stride or changing its basic posture. Then add a third rail.

$\mathcal{F}$inally a fourth and fifth rail (or cavalletto) can be added, and when the horse can do these perfectly, too, take the fourth rail away. Now you can build a little fence—crossed rails are fine—where the fifth rail was placed. The distance from the third rail will be nine to ten feet.

ALIX COLEMAN

*N*ext, you can build a little vertical, and after that a little square oxer. With the grid of cavalletti helping the horse always to find a perfect take-off spot, you can continue by building every kind of combination or gymnastic exercise you can think of, and teach the horse to cope with every kind of distance problem. Such exercises are wonderful for the rider, too.

ALIX COLEMAN

*T*he key to jumping big water jumps is to get high enough, and a rail in the middle of the water like this one at Hickstead is an excellent schooling aid. Snowbound (above) was probably the best water jumper I ever rode.

*K*sar d'Esprit was also no slouch over water. I think this form of water (at Aachen) with no takeoff at all is the most difficult of all, and invites the horse to jump too low and be careless. I would never school over such a water.

*J*umping *big walls takes a special technique and a very short stirrup. It is essential for the rider to really stay forward as the horse leaves the ground, and important to find, by trial and error, where the particular horse likes to leave from. (Above, Ksar d'Esprit at Toronto; below, First Boy at Aachen.)*

KARL SCHONERSTEDT

*F*leet Apple had a good bank-jumping technique, as he demonstrates here over the big bank at Hamburg. In the Spring Derby, a big vertical is placed just two strides away from the landing.

WEDDING & SOHN

*A*nother form of bank, this one at Aachen. There is a dry ditch at either end. Jumping a bank like this crosswise would be an ideal way to start the young horse.

*W*hatever you do, try to discourage the horse from leaping off into space from the very top, as Bold Minstrel had the audacity to do the first time he jumped Hickstead's big bank. Also, this is not how you should sit on a horse that is trying to spear itself, but I was caught completely by surprise!

problems if the initial foundation was sufficiently solid (and you shouldn't proceed to the next step until you're sure of that). The additional rails are placed at exactly the same spacing as was used for the first two rails. Now things become more interesting. (I should add that even the simplest exercises become challenging if you insist on doing them really correctly.)

At this point you remove the fourth rail and cross it with the fifth rail on a pair of standards. You now have a simple fence and the means of presenting your horse to it perfectly, because the cavalletti control the approach and the take-off point for you. Though I start here with crossed rails as the first fence, as soon as possible I like to substitute a little (three-foot) vertical and then a little (three feet by three feet) oxer. (I am not a big fan of crossed rails, for I believe they tend to make horses flat, or encourage them simply to step over instead of jumping, while the little oxer encourages horses to be round and use their backs.)

This basic setup—three cavalletti, a double space as a take-off spot and then a fence or a series of fences—is as useful for the show jumper and its rider as a batting tee is for a baseball player, or a ball machine for a tennis player—it enables you to practice the same move over and over until you groove it, and to work on pure technique. It also enables you to work on particular problems, and can be adapted to isolate almost any weakness. De Némethy has written a brilliant and comprehensive treatise on the use of this method and the infinite variations that can be applied to it (see Selected Bibliography), and it would be redundant for me to duplicate his labors here. Your own horse's weaknesses will suggest the variations that should be applied, but every horse must learn to deal with short distances, long distances and all the various combinations of long and short.

What does the rider do during these cavalletti exercises? They give him a wonderful opportunity to concentrate on his own technique as well, and to repeat each exercise until he can master it. The rider's principal role is to support, sustain and follow the horse's motion without anticipation. He rides through the cavalletti in a posting trot, balancing the horse between his aids. He maintains a perfect, even rein contact, while supporting the horse gently from behind with his legs. In the take-off area, he may add just a fraction of calf pressure as he sits, to offer the horse a little moral support; but he maintains exactly the same rein contact, and *must not "drop" the horse* by putting a lot of slack in the rein. (Incidentally, this is an ideal corrective exercise for riders who habitually "throw their horses away," or can't resist jumping themselves. I cannot overemphasize the fact that it's the horse that jumps; the rider simply goes with it. You don't have to make a little jump yourself.)

By continually varying the fences, strides and distances, you can avoid the principal pitfall of most technical work: boredom. Mindlessly repeating the same thing over and over is tiresome, and leads not to perfection but to sloppiness. The worst thing you can do is to keep practicing doing something wrong!

If you run into trouble at any point during your cavalletti and gymnastic work, the solution is simple: just go back a step or two, even all the way back to the single or double rails on the ground. For that matter, if you have a ground person to adjust the rails, it's a good idea to start right from the beginning every day at first, rapidly reviewing all of the previous stages. It isn't easy even for an experienced horse to start right off over a complex set of cavalletti and gymnastics, especially if it has a tendency to rush or anticipate. It's much better to start with the simple rail and add one element at a time. Simplify things by setting up a single, double and triple cavalletti grid somewhere on the riding ground away from the jumps you've put up for gymnastics. They can then be resorted to in your regular riding whenever you wish, or substituted for a trip over the gymnastic if your horse demonstrates signs of losing its confidence or composure.

Three-, four-, and even five-fence combinations can be built following the cavalletti grid, using varied striding, varied distances and varied types of fences (vertical, oxer, triple bar, etc.). Always start with normal distances, then gradually shorten or lengthen them according to your horse's particular schooling needs. A good progression for a triple combination of two three-foot-six-inch oxers and a four-foot vertical might run as follows: Start with a normal single stride and two normal strides to the vertical, say, twenty-three and thirty-two feet. (Because the fences are low, your "normal" distances will be on the short side of normal.) Then ask for a normal one stride, and two shorter strides, say, twenty-three and thirty feet; then a longer first stride and two longer strides, say, twenty-three and thirty-six feet; and finally a long first stride and two shorter strides, say, twenty-five and thirty-two feet.

As the horse progresses in this kind of work it should be able to handle one-stride distances from eighteen to twenty-seven feet, and two-stride distances from twenty-eight to thirty-seven feet, when the fences are about four feet high. It will, of course, be necessary to adjust the speed of your approach appropriately.

By varying the type and sequence of fences and the striding, you can expose a young horse to virtually every kind of combination over a three-month period, and it will learn to adjust its balance and the arc of its jump to virtually every circumstance.

What's missing in this sort of progression? The answer is obvious: only the approach to a single fence, unaided by cavalletti, and the problems posed by difficult lines.

I deal with the single fence by setting up a small isolated cross-rail as soon as the horse is jumping the cross-rail in the cavalletti well. Then I alternate trotting over the rail or rails on the ground and the single cross-rail (or later, a small vertical and/or small oxer). When the horse trots over the single small fence perfectly, I ask it to canter over the same small fences, never hurrying and never anticipating. (This means, above all, that the rider himself must not do these things.) If the horse persists in wanting to rush, I circle it as described in the next chapter.

When trotting over little fences, the rider should do a posting trot until the last two strides, when he should sit. When cantering over little fences, he should remain seated. Even when galloping over fences, the rider should ease into a full seat for the last two or three strides. I consider it a serious fault to ride the entire approach in a half-seat. First, because you can't influence the horse with your back if your seat is in the air; and then because you can't feel through your seat what the horse is doing or even exactly where it is. If the horse is thinking of stopping, you'll be slower to sense it in a half-seat, and even slower to do something about it. Moreover, while I wouldn't go so far as to say that riders have eyes in their seat, the "good eye for distance" often seems to be involved with a full seat, and riders who don't have it in a half-seat often seem to acquire an eye for distance when they sit.

Turns

Jumper courses consist of single fences and combinations of multiple fences jumped in a certain sequence, which constitutes the line or track of the course. Almost every jumper course incorporates at least two changes of direction, although hunter courses may be more straightforward. In the most difficult jumper courses, staying on a good line can be just as difficult as jumping the fences. The system described above should give the novice jumper a very good start in jumping single fences and every kind of combination, so it only remains to teach it about longer distances and difficult lines.

This can be started most easily by trotting and then cantering over rails on the ground arranged into simple courses. Most of the problems that may ensue when dealing with real fences at higher speeds will already reveal themselves here, where they can be dealt with in their simplest form.

The first real course for a green horse might be four three-foot-six-inch fences around the perimeter of the ring, perhaps with an oxer as the second fence and a little in-and-out as the fourth. You can very soon add a fence in the middle of the ring, or a diagonal line, so that the course can be readily reversed and jumped in either direction. (For that matter, most fences should be built so that they can be jumped both ways.) The distances between the two fences on each side should be very easy ones, using multiples of ten feet to adjust for the low fences and lower speed you'll prefer at the beginning, similar to the courses the horse will encounter during its show debut as a first-year green hunter.

Even an older horse that is doing its gymnastic work proficiently can benefit from cantering over more difficult lines using rails on the ground. I've never gone along with the idea that each horse has only so many jumps in it; but I do worry about boring them and see no point in jumping them needlessly. Practicing distance and turning problems and difficult lines over rails on the ground provides three quarters of the benefit of using real fences, without depleting the horse's energy. You can therefore do them more often, which is an added advantage. This sort of work is thus an ideal complement to schooling over real courses.

Schooling over huge fences is unnecessary even for older horses. De Némethy liked to point out to us that the great German teams of the 1930s rarely schooled over anything bigger than four feet six inches, and this was our practice at the USET Training Center in Gladstone, too. We'd try to jump little (four feet to four feet six inches) courses very accurately and perfectly, and we'd jump bigger fences only as a final school to "raise the horse's sights" before a show. Very occasionally, we'd keep building up the last fence of a gymnastic combination until it was of very respectable size, simply to test and develop the horse's scope and confidence. With this preparation, the bigger fences at the shows somehow took care of themselves. (If it *never* schools over anything big at home, seeing something much larger than it's accustomed to jumping for the first time at a show can be rather intimidating, even for the brave horse.)

Building courses for older horses is a matter of duplicating, more or less, the kind of course they will actually compete over at the shows. Schooling is schooling, and there should be no attempt to "wring them out" at home, but at the same time, all of the different kinds of challenges they will be expected to cope with in the show ring should be introduced and practiced. Your goal, ideally, is that the show horse can keep thinking as it approaches every new fence or combination on a Grand Prix course, "Oh yes, I recognize it, it's one of those," instead of constantly wondering, "What's this?"

It is particularly important to school over "option" distances (five and one-half, or six and one-half strides) and then to practice riding them both ways—in other words, both by adding the stride and by leaving it out. The solution you practice most should be the one that is less natural for the particular horse. ("Quick" horses that find it very easy to leave out a stride should mostly practice adding it, and vice versa.) A fuller discussion of all these more advanced matters will be found in Chapter 9, which deals with course walking and course strategy.

Schooling Jumpers at Liberty

An advantage of the method outlined in this chapter is that, in a pinch, you can do everything by yourself from the horse's back without any fancy facilities or even any help from the ground. However, it is also very helpful to complement under saddle work with some schooling in which the horse is obliged to perform entirely on its own initiative, and this can be accomplished in several different ways. A transitional form is to longe over rails on the ground, and then little cross-rails or oxers. Of course, the longer does retain a degree of control, so that the horse is not entirely independent, but it still does have to learn to make a lot of striding and take-off decisions on its own. The obvious disadvantage is simply that you are severely limited in the kinds of fences you can build on a short circle. Even so, you can teach the horse some useful things about figuring out strides to cavalletti and little fences on its own on the longe line.

Even better is what the horse can figure out for itself when it is truly at liberty in a corral or Hitchcock Pen, or a chute set up in an indoor ring. It is always best to give the horse a little "placing fence" to set up its striding as it comes into the chute or long side, but from that establishing point you can create whatever training program you think your horse can use: combinations, related distances, tests of scope or whatever. Do be careful not to lay real traps for the horse, or build fences of a size that will undermine rather than strengthen its confidence in its own ability; but short of that, you can teach the horse a lot and learn a lot about it by watching it as well.

_____ *Eight* _____

SOLVING
JUMPER
PROBLEMS

*T*he beauty of the method out-
lined in the last chapter is the fact that it is so completely progressive that it gives you an almost automatic
solution to most training problems: you simply go backward down the scale of progression until you reach the
point at which the problem no longer exists, and you start
again from there.

There are a few stubborn cases, however, which cannot be dealt with in this way: for example, the horse that
does its cavalletti and gymnastic work well but still wants
to rush or pick up speed over a course; the horse that
stops or runs out without warning; the horse that has a

problem with water jumps and ditches; and the horse that knocks down too many fences through sheer careless-ness. Let's examine some of these, starting with the horse that insists on rushing.

There are lots of ways to deal with hot horses that don't even involve schooling techniques *per se*, and you'll find a discussion of these measures in Chapter 10. Most of them are merely aids to a solution, not complete or per-manent solutions in themselves. For habitual rushers, there is no better cure than repeatedly making long approaches to a fence and circling away from it the moment the horse ruins the approach by attempting to rush.

Take the case of a horse that works well over cavalletti, trots and canters well over rails on the ground and even over cross-rails, but still wants to rush or anticipate when it jumps a bigger single fence on a real course. The rem-edy for this is to start an approach, and then make a big circle the instant the horse blows its cool, only to return to the same approach. You may have to make five, ten or even more circles before you ever let the horse jump the fence; and you may then have to circle in the other direc-tion another ten times before its approach is good enough for you to permit it to jump again. It's a long process that takes a lot of patience; but it's the only technique that really works—provided, of course, that you don't spoil it by rushing too—in other words, by deciding arbitrarily to jump after the next approach, whether or not it's any good.

Never forget that the point of circling is to practice making approaches. When you're on the line to a fence, if you don't straighten out your circles enough to hold the horse in a straight approach for three or four strides, or if the circles are too small to permit the horse to settle back into a good gait before returning to the line to the fence, then they'd serve no useful purpose. Circling is not just a matter of whipping around a few times and then charging at the fence!

Actually, your circle before a fence should not be perfectly round, but shaped more or less like a racetrack with a true straightaway. True circles "telegraph" your intentions, and when you finally straighten out the line, the horse knows for sure that it's going to jump. More oval circles, on the other hand, raise a question in its mind whenever you straighten them: "Am I going to be asked to jump this time or not?" Eventually the horse will learn that the answer is "Yes" only when the approach is perfect, and sometimes not even then.

Some trainers think it's all right to let the horse canter the last stride or two when trotting over fences, but I do not agree. Trotting is trotting, and breaking into a canter is another form of hurrying or anticipating. So I always try to discourage this with my fingers. I'll even go back to lower fences or rails on the ground until the trot is perfectly maintained. When horses insist on breaking only in the very last stride, however, I let them get away with it and then try to correct it the next time. The reason for this is that you don't want to introduce any confusion in the horse's mind between circling at the very last minute, and turning just slightly in order to angle the fence or to set up a turn you want to make immediately on landing.

As we have noted, spoiled horses and naturally "quick" ones often tend to raise their heads as they approach a set of cavalletti or a fence. With them, it's not a bad idea at the beginning to let your hand drift almost imperceptibly higher on a soft rein before steadying the horse more actively. Often a very gentle vibration at this point is sufficient to stabilize the trot and keep the horse from rushing or breaking. In fact, the ability to anticipate and block the horse's evasion before its intention is expressed in action is one of the distinguishing characteristics of a good rider. Good riders always seem to deal with problems before they really get started; while the less skillful always seem surprised by what was obviously about to happen.

You may have noticed that one of the techniques I do *not* advocate is pulling up, or pulling up and backing, in front of the fence. I want my horses to know that as long as they are headed at the fence, they're going to jump it unless I turn away. I may tell them to "Wait, wait, wait"; but they have to believe that I always intend to jump the fence unless I turn them away from it. If they start second-guessing and say to themselves, "I bet he's going to pull me up this time," you may not be able to start them up again quickly enough to avoid a bad fence or a refusal. I can't count the number of important classes I've seen lost in just this way, because perfectly well-meaning horses simply misread the rider's intention.

Spoiled horses with an ingrained tendency to rush often benefit from jumping a complete course of fences with circling interpolated between almost every two fences. You jump the first fence and approach the second, but you circle when you get there. Every time the horse has jumped a fence there should be another one in front of him, preferably quite a way off (ten strides is fine, fifteen even better). He's always looking at the next fence, but at the beginning of his reschooling, you'll never ask him to jump it until he is completely relaxed. Eventually, the horse learns that there's no point in getting all excited whenever it sees a fence because it probably won't jump it anyway.

At this point, you can start jumping whole lines and finally whole courses, circling before only one or two jumps.

Next to cavalletti and gymnastic work, I've found this technique to be more useful in retraining hot horses than all the others put together.

Run-outs and Refusals

Some of the most frequent rerun scenarios on the horse show circuit go like this:

- A junior hunter comes into the ring and makes a circle, with no impulsion at all, "going nowhere." It's been standing at the in-gate for fifteen minutes in the hot sun and is half-asleep. The horse plods down to the first fence and stops. The rider pats the horse and tries the fence again. The horse stops again.
- A junior hunter, this one full of beans, jumps the first fence with so much *brio* that it leaves out a stride at the second. The rider doesn't check but starts turning, late, toward the third fence. The horse never gets straight and runs out. The rider pats the horse and comes back to the fence on the same line. The horse runs out again.

- An amateur-owner jumper jumps fence three and heads for the Liverpool. This particular horse isn't sure that it likes Liverpools, so the rider kicks it extra hard and tries to help it off the ground with a big "crest release." The horse stops and the rider lands in the Liverpool. Suspecting that his horse is laughing at him, the rider gets back on and jerks its mouth.

I shudder to think of how many times I've seen these scenarios enacted in real life. Yet all are essentially irrational and unnecessary.

Refusals and run-outs are a sort of body language too. What is the horse telling you? It's usually saying, "On the basis of the ride you gave me, I did the most natural thing." But the message may sometimes be more precise: "I didn't have much impulsion and didn't feel like it." "I got to an impossible spot from which to jump." "I don't like that kind of fence." "I get afraid when I see water." "I saw something that distracted me." "It's too big for me." "No, I don't want to."

How should the rider handle such problems? First, I would make a distinction between a refusal and a run-out: the refuser actually stops and thus says "no," while the horse that runs out keeps going but contrives to avoid jumping the fence.

In the case of a refusal for whatever reason—even justifiable ones—my first action is to spank the horse. Refusing is totally unacceptable behavior for a jumper under almost any circumstance, and it's important that the horse should understand this. (I use the word "spanking" because that's what it should be, not a euphemism for "whipping," which it should *not* be.) The spanking is not intended to cause pain, although it should be distinctly uncomfortable, not merely a couple of timid love pats. It must also be immediate, so that the horse can have no doubt whatsoever as to what it did to provoke it. And it should surprise, embarrass, chagrin and discourage the horse from repeating that behavior. It should also be of very brief duration. (You should be finished long before the audience or judges start to get upset.)

Never abuse the horse's mouth, and *never* hit it around

the head. Three or four good whacks on the rump should be plenty. After that, you can pat it if you wish, as part of the reorganization process. Then come back to the fence in perfect control, and do *not* change your riding. If horses will only jump for you when you're kicking and whipping, you're in deep trouble; they have to go when you are riding normally. Whatever you do, don't make a big crest release or anticipate the next takeoff. All the congenital refusers, the "dirty" refusers who have the idea always lurking in their mind, are just waiting for you to drop them so that they can refuse.

In a run-out, where speed is part of the problem, it's seldom a good idea to spank the horse. The important thing is to come back to the fence from the side to which the horse ran out. For example, if it ran out to the right, you should try the fence the next time on a slight angle coming from right to left, which would make another run-out to the right very difficult to execute. Again, if you refuse to drop the horse's head, it will jump the fence nine times out of ten.

The AHSA and FEI Rule Books wisely allow you to make only three public displays of your problem (three refusals) before eliminating you from the show ring. In this event, I'd pick any easy fence and jump it on the way out, so that the horse does not leave the ring on a refusal. Then try to solve your problem outside. The show ring is the worst place in which to try to reform a stopper.

What about refusals that take place even while schooling at home? Ideally, all of your problems should be dealt with there, never in public. Most of the refusals and run-outs in the above scenarios resulted from poor preparation or a poor approach, and the obvious solution to them is simply not to make bad approaches. The "I don't want to" kind of refusal is something else, for this can sometimes occur after a perfectly adequate approach. The only way to eliminate this kind of stop is to remind the horse from time to time that a refusal will trigger immediate, just retribution. You often see this kind of horse being ridden very aggressively, with the rider trying hard to prevent it from stopping, but I don't believe that riding aggressively is the answer. Instead, I'd prefer to build a rather unattractive fence, and ride down to it a bit halfheartedly. Do not *ask* the horse to stop, but create a situation in which a horse with stopping in its mind is practically bound to do so. *Then* spank it, hard. You should afterward be able to ride back to the fence normally, without whipping or spurring, and find that the horse jumps it willingly. This is just what you want: to be able to ride normally, confident that the horse will go. It's impossible to ride well if you're always trying to prevent a stop. Confirmed stoppers—horses that are constantly on the lookout for a chance to cheat—should be sold or traded, unless you are a true masochist who enjoys suffering. They can be real heartbreakers.

With a green horse, the only kinds of refusals that are fairly excusable are those involving a strange fence it hasn't seen before, or a fence that looks big enough to shake its confidence. Theoretically, such refusals should never occur if new fences are always introduced in the right way and if the size is increased only very gradually from a thoroughly established base of confidence.

I like to introduce new fences in a very simple form, no higher than three feet six inches. Before I ever ride down to one, I let the green horse smell it and examine it at some length. Then I trot down to it very determinedly, and jump it two or three times from both sides. I'm even willing to let the horse break into a canter the last stride or two, if it's very keen to jump. The fence is so low that I can almost always force the horse over the first time; but if it stops, I spank it and come back to the fence again. After all, the horse has had a chance to examine the fence and that's all I let it have, since it will have to jump many strange fences in the show ring without a formal introduction. I consider it a big mistake to permit a jumper to stop at any fence that looks a bit peculiar, because peculiar-looking fences are going to be part of its experience as long as it lives. And when it's headed at a fence it should always be thinking, *"How* am I going to jump this fence," and never "Do I feel like jumping this fence?"

If the fence looks big to the horse, and if I think its refusal was due to lack of self-confidence, I'll still spank it for stopping, but I'll then put the fence down and let it jump this easier version a couple of times. Invariably, when you raise it again, the horse will jump it—provided that you've raised it three inches and not a foot. Every horse has its limitations. If a horse consistently struggles over four feet six inches and stops at four feet nine inches and five feet, I'd conclude that it is basically a four-foot-six horse and forget about a jumper career for it.

Water and Ditches

Another understandable kind of stopping involves water and ditches, with which some horses never become entirely comfortable. Their wariness may even be a good thing, since horses that become too comfortable with water tend to jump into it a lot. Most of the great water jumpers I've known hated to get their feet wet; left to their own devices, they'd probably never have jumped water at all.

Why do certain horses have problems with water and ditches? Let me give you another scenario: the next show on your schedule is likely to have some water jumps, so you decide to give your horse a school over water beforehand. You improvise a bad water jump with a scruffy takeoff and a landing tape that's practically invisible. The horse is shown the fence (which is only about ten feet wide between the wings and almost that same distance from takeoff to landing) and you ride down to it. The horse stops, gets spanked and then is run at the fence at a higher rate of speed. It jumps this a couple of times, and then someone says, "Now let's see if it will jump the *regular* water"—meaning a twelve-footer. This time the horse jumps smack in the middle of it, gets spanked again and so forth and so forth. While I have seen this scenario enacted many times, in many versions, I consider it the antithesis of rational behavior.

What procedure would I recommend instead? First of all, I think of the water not as just another fence, but as a very special kind of fence requiring an entirely different technique from any ordinary vertical or spread.

Whether or not a horse has a special talent for jump-

*T*he habit of "dropping" horses—losing contact with their mouth as they leave the ground—makes it very difficult to jump fences at an angle, or to turn immediately upon landing. However, taking the shortest line is still the best way to win against the clock. (Above, Snowbound at Aachen; below, Sinjon in the "old" Fiftieth Street Madison Square Garden.)

*T*he best jumpers have great freedom of the shoulder, enabling them to get their knees very high and very forward, right under the throatlatch, as the four brilliant horses on this and the facing page are doing. (Above, Riviera Wonder in the 1960 Rome Olympics; below, Ksar d'Esprit at White City, London.)

UDO SCHMIDT

*W*hen horses are making this kind of effort, the worst thing the rider can do is to "stiff" them by not getting forward enough, and it has always felt very natural to me to leave the knee angle quite open to preclude this. *(Above, Bold Minstrel at Aachen; below, Snowbound in the 1968 Mexico City Olympics.)*

WERNER ERNST

*T*hough it is certainly desirable for horses to have a perfect technique with their knees, it is not absolutely essential if they get their body high enough. First Boy's knees were rarely much tighter than this, but he was still good enough to win the George V Gold Cup at London and a lot of other classes.

*S*nowbound was not quite classical with his knees either, for his most natural instinct was to unfold very early. However, trying to change him wouldn't have made much sense, and we let him do things his own way.

UDO SCHMIDT

*W*hen horses are struggling to jump really huge fences, I'd rather see riders follow their instincts and try to help instead of worrying too much about details of position and looking pretty. (Above, Main Spring at Aachen; below, Ksar d'Esprit winning the second phase of the World Championships at Venice in 1960.)

L'ANNÉE HIPPIQUE

*T*his is what a real "safety" seat looks like: Pat Taaffe and the three-time Grand National winner Arkle, running in the 1966 Cheltenham Gold Cup. Taaffe wasn't sure Arkle would stand up, and wasn't going to risk coming off the front end; but Arkle hardly changed expression, and they won.

*T*his looks like a safety-seat situation as well, and getting a rail between your legs (as Fleet Apple is about to do) is one of the better ways of standing on your head! As it was, he somehow managed to stand up.

L'ANNÉE HIPPIQUE

*C*ould either of these two horses jump? It's hard to tell when they're standing still, but Raimondo d'Inzeo's Merano (above) was certainly one of the most brilliant horses of his generation, while Bold Minstrel (below) won Games medals both in eventing and jumping, and could do just about anything. Both horses were well into their teens when these pictures were taken.

U.S. EQUESTRIAN TEAM

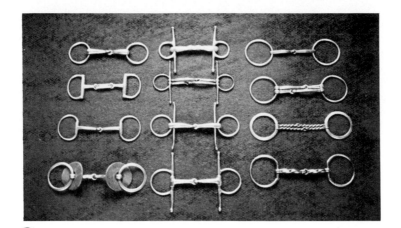

A variety of snaffles of different patterns and sizes; there is something here that would suit most horses. The only bit I don't like is the "fat" snaffle at top left; the ring is small enough to make almost any head look plain. The full cheek to its right has a composition mouth that comes in different flavors! The double twisted wire next to the bottom on the right looks more severe than it is, and many horses go well in it.

ALIX COLEMAN

T his is what I consider correct adjustment of the running martingale. When the horse's head is in the correct place there is no effect at all, but if the head rises very far, the martingale starts to inhibit the evasion. Note the ring stops to prevent the martingale from hanging up where the rein joins the bit.

*R*iding a sensitive little horse like Touch of Class is not easy if you're well over six feet tall, for you have to ride short and work hard to fold up very smoothly and neatly. Joe Fargis's reward for learning to do all these things very well indeed was an individual gold medal at the Los Angeles Olympics in 1984.

*T*he silver medalist right on Fargis's heels in 1984 was Conrad Homfeld with Abdullah, and both shared the team gold medal as well. I cannot recall ever seeing two riders produce more stylish performances when the chips were down, the style not being pasted on as an end in itself, but purely a by-product of soundly effective function.

*T*wo prime examples of what the Europeans regard as an inexhaustible supply of brilliant U.S. lady riders. Between them Leslie Burr Lenehan (above on Siriska) and Katie Monahan Prudent (below on Nordic Venture) have won four American Grandprix Association Rider of the Year and five AGA Horse of the Year awards, and team gold medals in the Pan American and Olympic Games (Lenehan) and the World Championships (Prudent). If they're doing anything wrong, it obviously isn't very critical!

BOB LANGRISH

A beautiful, economical style doesn't necessarily have to come at the expense of energy or determination to win, and nobody demonstrates that better or more consistently than Michael Matz, seen here on Chef at Aachen, where they anchored our gold-medal team in the World Championships in 1986. Also a Pan American Games individual gold medalist (with Jet Run in 1979), a winner of the World Cup Finals (1981), and a bronze individual medalist in the World Championships (1978), Matz is notable for having achieved success with a very wide range of horses, something not even great riders can always do.

*I*n 1984 at the Los Angeles Olympic Games, French star Pierre Durand surely experienced one of Life's Darkest Moments, looking at Jappeloup from the other side of the fence with the bridle in his hands! European Champion three years later with the same fabulous little horse, and Olympic gold medalist at Seoul (where the above picture was taken) the following year, Pierre has the sympathy and inspiration to catch lightning in a bottle! His riding is certainly not mechanical, and sometimes not even very orthodox, but Pierre and Jappeloup understand each other perfectly, and truly form an indivisible partnership.

*S*ilver medalists at Seoul both individually and in the team were
young (then twenty-one) Greg Best and Gem Twist, who form together
another highly individualistic and dazzlingly brilliant partnership. But if
Jappeloup's "thing" is to bounce like a rubber ball, Gem Twist's is to run
and jump, leaving out two strides where even the scopiest horses are
struggling to leave out one. There is more to this than just the confidence
of youth, for Greg is not only a very sound rider mechanically, but also
benefits from the tactical advice of Frank Chapot, a six-time Olympian who
bred Gem and rode his sire unforgettably.

*C*anada's Ian Millar and Big Ben are another unforgettable collaboration between a horse and rider that seem perfectly suited to each other. Though Ian must have been sorely tempted to force Ben's development before the Los Angeles Olympics, he patiently built a really sound foundation instead, and was rewarded by becoming the first rider to win World Cup Finals titles back to back in 1988 and 1989. The picture above, taken at Gothenburg on the occasion of the first title, is entirely characteristic and entirely correct, showing perfect contact, perfect balance and complete sympathy.

*M*ost impressive of the younger generation of West German riders is
Franke Sloothaak, seen here winning the Grand Prix of Stockholm in
1989 on Waltzerkoenig, on which he had earlier won the Grand Prix of
Aachen. The picture reflects Franke's complete confidence as he jumped
the last fence; with a perfect distance and a horse that was jumping
very round and very clean, he simply sat in perfect balance and "loose-
reined" Waltzerkoenig to encourage him to use himself freely
and confidently.

*N*ot perhaps quite as orthodox stylistically as some of his peers—he
doesn't worry much about his lower leg—England's John Whitaker has
forged one of the most consistent partnerships in show jumping history
with Milton, his mount in winning the European individual title in 1989,
the World Cup title in 1990, and innumerable Grand Prix. Nobody
clocks a horse down to a fence more accurately than John, whose
steadiness and coolness under pressure belie his ability to produce
dazzling jump-off times, yet without ever appearing to hurry.

ing really difficult water is so much a matter of chance that I've sometimes wondered if it's quite fair to judge faults at the tape at all; perhaps every water jump should have rails, and only faults at the rail should be counted. With things as they are, I like to start by reducing the water to its very simplest form, just as we reduced the ordinary fence to a single rail on the ground. And my simplest form of "water" would be a dry ditch, twelve feet wide from wing to wing, about two and a half to three feet deep, and three to four feet wide. I'd put wings on both sides of this ditch and give the horse a lead over it the first time or two. By the end of the first school, the horse should have acquired quite a lot of confidence about jumping ditches from a trot and canter, which is the beginning of a water-jumping technique. If the horse happens to land a trailing leg a bit short, it will learn a valuable lesson: don't land short!

You can see that my philosophy in dealing with jumper problems is consistent with the way I try to solve problems on the flat. You try to elicit behavior that you can reward, if possible the very first time, and never repeat (thus practice) the behavior you *don't* want. You try to create a "can't lose" situation in which you are most likely to get the horse to do the right thing, however awkwardly, the very first time or two. You can always smooth it out later. What you have to avoid at all cost is to attempt something in so difficult a form that you cannot possibly get immediate compliance, and then to wage a pitched battle by refusing to back off and present the challenge in a simpler, easier form.

Once the dry ditch has been mastered, you can move on to a real water jump (six feet wide is plenty, five feet even better), constructed so that there is a perceptible "lip" on the landing side, maybe three inches deep, and well padded. If you use one of the temporary rubber water jumps, you can achieve the same effect by digging a hole and placing the rubber "pool" in it. At first, I'd jump it by itself, then quickly add a take-off brush and a rail partway across.

Once the horse is jumping a narrow span of water consistently, confidently and in good form, you can move on to a wider one, eight or ten feet wide. I think it's no more useful or necessary to jump big waters of twelve to fifteen feet at home than it is to jump a lot of five-foot schooling fences. Unless a horse has exceptional natural talent for jumping water—which is to say that it gets good height over the water without any particular inducement —I'd always school with a rail or two over the water in order to encourage the horse to jump consistently high enough. Paradoxically, the key to broad jumps for horses, as for human athletes, is *height*. Left to their own devices, too many horses become very casual about jumping over water (for the fence invites carelessness); and since a foot on the tape costs you just as many faults as a rail carried on the horse's chest, any little extra precaution you can take to ensure its continued interest in jumping the water cleanly is a good investment.

Banks

Banks are more difficult psychologically than techni-cally. Of all the "impressive" fences, they are technically the easiest to negotiate. It's always possible to scramble up any bank somehow or other, and once on top of it, every horse will eventually find some way to get down again. So the key to jumping banks, as in everything else, is simply to start with a bank that is reduced to its sim-plest terms: three feet to three feet six inches high with room for one or two strides on top. Once the horse's basic technique has been soundly established complexity can be added, and it can be asked to try a bigger bank, say, one that is four feet high, perhaps with a step to a higher level, and then a bigger drop on the landing side. Very often this will be the same bank, negotiated from a different direction.

Banks have to be ridden relatively aggressively, so that the horse doesn't get into the habit of being so care-ful on top that it fails to get the striding right. You want it to be careful only when coming off the top of a really big bank (like those at Hamburg and Hickstead); then the slower you descend the better, provided that the horse, in hesitating at the edge, doesn't take a step backward and thus incur three faults. If a vertical fence follows on the landing side (as it frequently does), you may wish to angle it in order to give yourself a bit more room; two strides straight ahead usually result in a front knockdown. If your horse should happen to descend a big bank too quickly, don't hesitate to slip your reins and adopt a real "safety" seat. Many riders come off over the horse's shoulder if its knees buckle on landing.

Dealing with a Careless Jumper

In my earlier book *Riding and Jumping*, I devoted several pages to discussing various forms of rapping and related techniques designed to make a careless horse try harder, not because I have a fixation on the subject (as certain innocents have alleged), but because rapping was, is and always will be a fact of the show jumper's life. Why? Because most of these methods for getting horses to jump more cleanly actually work, in varying degrees, and thus lead to more clear rounds, more blue ribbons and more money. Are they intrinsically cruel? Not if employed with intelligence and discretion. And so, despite all the legislation aimed at limiting or prohibiting these practices, despite the fact that they are abhorred by sincere if misguided animal activists and muckraking journalists and despite the fact that they are subject to abuse by morons (who abuse everything they touch anyway), many riders will continue to use them. Good horsemen, moreover, will employ them very skillfully and judiciously, and their competitive results and often their horses' training as well will benefit very significantly.

The principle behind poling is simple: if you stub your toe on something once, you tend to be more careful the next time. The various forms of poling arrange for the horse to "stub its toe" when it makes its habitual casual effort, and thus reminds it to put out a bit more the next time. The commonest ways of arranging for an educational bump are by sharply raising some sort of pole so that it raps the horse's shin or coronet just at the peak of its arc over a vertical fence; or by offsetting a bamboo pole or a thin piece of iron pipe on the takeoff or landing side of a fence by placing it a foot or two wide of the top element of the fence, and at the same height or slightly higher.

The International Equestrian Federation has, for twenty years, forbidden all kinds of rapping whatsoever while horses are under its jurisdiction; at our national shows the American Horse Shows Association permits supervised manual poling with a two-inch, taped bamboo, and also permits the bamboo to be offset on one side or the other of a fence in "passive poling," in which the horse hits itself. My observation has been that the AHSA, by permitting two practices which are difficult to abuse, has markedly reduced covert reliance on more seriously abusive practices, and minimized the hypocrisy that has often existed under FEI rules. However, the FEI is unlikely to change its position in the foreseeable future, except to make its rules and penalties even stiffer. So the jumper rider finds himself with an additional problem: how to stay within the rules and still get an occasionally careless horse to leave up enough fences in order to win in this era of light rails and shallow cups.

Because so little can be done within the rules at the show grounds, especially at international competitions, more and more riders must learn to rely on what can be done at home between shows, and on the horse's basic jumping training. The technique I am most reluctant to use (even though it's permitted by the AHSA) is manual poling. Few people have the hand-eye coordination, quick wrists and judgment to do it really well; and it requires someone to be standing by the schooling fence who will not be present in the show ring. Horses are amazingly sharp about noticing things like that. Besides, once they've been hit a time or two, many horses become reluctant to go down to the fence at all if there's someone standing beside it, unless they are ridden very aggressively; and if they start refusing, they'd be better off if they'd been left in the barn.

In schooling jumpers, it is vitally important to cherish and preserve the careful jumper's interest in jumping fences cleanly right from the outset of its career, and to stimulate and reinforce the careless horse's latent instinct of self-preservation by never letting it find out that the vast majority of fences are incapable of biting back. In the case of the careful horse, we must guard against dulling its interest through mindless repetition of simple, boring exercises. In the case of the duller one, we must shield it from the knowledge that many fences in the world actually fall down very easily, by avoiding such fences during its daily schooling.

In the old days, many cavalry schools taught their horses to respect the fences (at the same time saving themselves the trouble of resetting them) by doing a lot of schooling over fences that were absolutely fixed and solid, and even over "rails" that were actually iron pipes. There was a lot of wasted horse talent, but the survivors acquired a very healthy respect for fences and tried to jump anything that was put in their way, even if they had to do it off one leg.

Today, the risks of injury to valuable horses are far too high even to consider such practices. However, there are available alternatives that are almost as effective and infinitely safer, in the form of cups of variable depth with which to support the rails. Shallow cups, which support the rail to less than one third of its diameter, are useful in actual competition as the top rail of a "bogey" vertical, or as the far rail of a very wide spread. But at home they're useless, since they can teach the horse the very thing we don't want it to know: that some fences will fall at the lightest touch and won't sting a bit.

I prefer cups on schooling fences to be the so-called "deep" cups that support the rail to just under one half of its diameter. And for congenitally careless horses that continually rub or knock down fence after fence without batting an eye, I like to have several three-quarter-inch (outside diameter) iron pipes, at least one of them painted white, to place on top of fences that usually invite a hit. (Since I use mostly round rails, I usually simply rest an extra pair of shallow cups on top of the top rail, and place the pipe on them.) Hitting one of these makes a resounding noise and seems to sting and surprise the horse much more than rubbing a rail; but if it jumps the fence cleanly, nothing happens.

In my opinion, this method is more likely to develop consistently clean jumping than any other; and if your horse is habitually pretty clean, you don't need to do anything special when you get to a show, because trying not to hit fences has become its way of life. I can think of only one horse I've ever had that was totally impervious to the effect of the pipe. (In fact, it would ring it like a gong, over and over again, and finally ended up as a hack instead of a jumper.) The only thing to do with compulsively careless horses (as with compulsively dangerous ones) is to trade or sell them as soon as you're convinced of their incorrigible flaw.

Of course, there are many other ways of dealing with careless horses. Some riders will build a biggish fence and simply put a horse so wrong to it that a wreck is unavoidable. And since it's hard (as well as illegal) to set up a "bump" at a show run under international rules, it's not unusual to see riders who have a fence down in the ring then deliberately run through two or three more, hoping that the horse will be more careful the next time. I abhor these practices, as I think you should *never* lie to your horse by encouraging it to jump or demanding that it jump from a spot from which it hasn't got a chance of making it. Moreover, there's the risk—call it poetic justice—that if you lie to your horse too often, it is very apt to learn to lie to you in return.

Correcting Faults in Jumping Form

The basic instinctive jumping style and mechanism that horses are born with is usually theirs for life; but certain flaws can be corrected to some extent by carefully selected gymnastic exercises and by the use of offsets in schooling. Again, I don't really recommend attempting to accomplish this through manual poling (although I've seen it done, and very skillfully, by several artists of another age). But you can accomplish just as much far more safely by using passive poling with some form of offset.

What precisely are you trying to achieve? Well, by offsetting something *in* on the horse (in other words, by placing a bamboo, an iron pipe or a strand of baling wire level with the top of a low fence—four feet maximum—and about two feet on the takeoff side), you will encourage the horse to snap its knees earlier and tighter and to jump a bit higher. If you install the same offset on the landing side, you will encourage the horse to be tighter and/or a bit higher with its hindquarters, and to stay in the air a little longer without "cutting down" on the fence.

And if you do this with some discretion and not on every other fence (which eventually tends to make the horse back off) you can get the horse to use this tighter technique pretty consistently. Of course, short oxer combinations (say, over fences three feet six inches square and with an inside spacing of twenty-one feet) accomplish pretty much the same thing.

What is the best choice between bamboo, pipe and wire? Whichever offset you prefer, you will be wise to use a separate pair of standards instead of the brackets that were customary when offsets were legal under FEI Rules. The bamboo and the pipe are simply rested in shallow cups; the wire is fixed at one end but attached with only a half twist at the other, so that it readily comes loose. The offset bamboo is foolproof but fairly visible, the offset pipe capable of putting a knee on a horse if it should happen to hit it just wrong. I think it is impossible to hurt a horse at all if wire is used as recommended. Its effect is mostly psychological, since the horse hits some little thing it hasn't even seen, and simply gives the whole fence a little more leeway the next time. However, the greater convenience of using the other forms of offset usually dictate their use for most people. (And somehow, they sound less sinister, even though wire is actually the mildest of the three.)

Whatever form of barrage or rapping you employ, you must always remember that the limiting factor will be each particular horse's individual temperament and threshold of pain. (Some horses just rub a fence and instantly sharpen up, while others can run through a telephone pole without batting an eye.) Six-time Olympic rider Frank Chapot likes to point out that courage and carefulness are often inversely related and warns that as you make the horse more careful, it may become reluctant even to attempt a fence it is not sure it can jump cleanly. Very careful, very clean jumpers may have some "chicken" in them for this very reason, and preserving their confidence is so important that with this kind of horse you may be better off doing no sharpening at all. (Abstinence also enables you to chide all the people who have careless horses to cope with, at least until you get one yourself.)

Even with the average horse, it is easy to do too much—to get it hit so often that it starts to back off from its fences and compels you to alter your riding style. Thus it is terribly important, in schooling, for you to learn when enough is enough (and often it is not very much), and to know when to stop. Remember, you sharpen in order to correct the error of carelessness, and if that error isn't there when you start, everything you do will hurt rather than help your show-ring performance.

Head Flippers

A particularly annoying habit some horses acquire as a result of being ridden by someone with bad hands, who hits them in the mouth while jumping, is flipping their heads (snapping them upward) as they strike the ground on landing. In most cases, they'll also do it when negotiating rails on the ground at a canter, and it should be corrected then. If not, there is an absolutely specific remedy: trotting and cantering over low single fences in draw reins run between the front legs.

I should, however, add a warning: even though I've never seen or experienced it myself, I've been told that horses can get tangled up in draw reins rigged like this, and fall. I can't quite imagine how this could happen *over little fences*, any more than I can imagine horses getting hung up in running martingales and falling (which is something else I've heard about but never seen). This being said, only fairly advanced riders who have an absolutely steady hand and completely independent aids should employ this remedial technique.

Here is how this procedure works: when the horse performs the act of jumping with the draw reins run between its front legs, it shortens the distance between its mouth and the girth, thus relieving pressure on the bit instead of adding to it on leaving the ground and while in the air. If the horse flips its head on landing, it simply hits itself, and most horses are quick to figure this out. In fact, I've never seen this problem take very long to solve provided that there's no abuse of the horse's mouth while the horse is leaving the ground or in the air.

Overbending

Riding literature is full of dire warnings against the danger of overbending: when the horse bends its neck instead of its poll, and draws its nose very far inside the vertical. And rightly so, for a horse that learns to put its head on its chest and pull from there can often evade the action of the rider's hands and do whatever it likes.

Then why do so many jumpers seem to spend so much time in draw reins when they're not on course, often with the draw reins run between their front legs, practically forcing their heads between their knees? In many a prize-awarding ceremony, half the winning horses, carrying some of the best-known riders in the world, are seen following this practice. The answer is that if a jumper rider has to choose between overbending and underbending, overbending is the lesser evil, in that the horse at least stays round. Furthermore, some riders "don't have the time" (and others, let's face it, don't have the knowledge) to put their horse's heads in place by any other means. I'm not a great believer of draw reins used to the extreme because coercive solutions are seldom permanent; and in this case, the horses are merely given an incentive to get even when they are finally free to raise their heads.

But fortunately, it's usually quite easy to correct a horse that has gotten into the habit of overbending. The rider simply pushes one or both hands as far forward as possible, and gives the horse's mouth a relatively sharp, upward bump, starting with a slack rein. (This is the only circumstance in which I'd ever put slack in a rein before making it active.) Usually this action shouldn't have to be repeated many times, provided that the rider has good hands and can make the horse comfortable once its head carriage is correct.

Coping with "Comfort Stops"

This seems a funny thing to write about, but one of the more foolish practices riders get into the habit of indulging is to stop every time the horse feels like emptying itself. The problem is that the horse begins to think of this as an inalienable right, and then one day, on the way to the first fence of an important class, the horse gets the urge. "No, *this* time you have to keep moving," says the rider; but it's too late. The horse's mind is elsewhere.

During a long career I've seen literally dozens of classes lost this way, including some very important ones. So I've always made it a practice to teach my horses to keep going and do what they have to do on the run, so to speak. And they all learn to do it.

Horses that Jump to the Corner

This is often a physical problem rather than a riding problem. In my experience, horses that jump to the corner of a fence usually have something that hurts when they land, even though they may appear to jog out soundly. (Very often the problem eventually shows up in the form of heat or lameness.) So I usually seek the solution elsewhere than in specific schooling techniques.

When no physical symptoms can be found to account for this tendency, and if the rider is convinced that it's simply a bad habit the horse has developed, he might find a remedy of sorts in jumping fences with a "V" of sloping rails resting on top, the rails coming to an apex where they rest on the top rail of the vertical fence, and being spread eight or ten feet apart on the ground at the take-off side. Normally, the apex of the "V" will be right in the middle of the fence; as you can imagine, the ever-narrowing distance between the rails will discourage the horse from jumping in the corner or, for that matter, staying on the ground too long. (In this respect, the "V" acts rather like an offset, in that it encourages the horse to snap its knees a bit earlier.) I've never found the "V" to be a panacea, but I know some good horsemen who use it constantly, so the chances are that it has some value.

Some Practical Advice on Building Fences

The final jumping recommendations I'd like to offer don't actually involve horse problems, but are of concern to people who work with jumpers and have to build the fences they jump.

Everyone involved with jumpers ought to know something about building fences. During a long career, you'll build a lot of them, and if you get into the habit of doing it in the most practical and labor-saving way early on, it will save you untold effort over the years. A good way to learn what's most practical is to volunteer to serve on a horse show jump crew for an afternoon or two. You'll never again pick up a standard wrong side up and see all the pins fall out on the ground!

For much of my riding life I've been blessed by having experienced people to do a lot of the fence moving, especially with the USET (although Bert de Némethy usually conscripted both grooms and riders to do the work of building courses in the afternoons). More recently, I've had to share indoor rings and schooling grounds with others, many of whom really have no idea of the most rudimentary principles of fence building. So let me review a few good basic practices:

- Set up your standards in matching pairs, and always move and adjust them a pair at a time. Otherwise, when you build square oxers (and you ought to build a lot of them) the heights will never match. By matching pairs I mean that the standards should match in height, the cups should match, there should be at least three cups on each standard and all the pins should be inserted from the same direction. Pins should be inserted just far enough to penetrate the far side of the bracket. Pushing them all the way through makes them more awkward to remove, while pushing them through only one side tips the cup, will bend the pin if the fence is hit hard and is simply lazy.

- Even if a cup is not in use (because you're building only a single rail, or have only a single rail on the far side of an oxer, for example) *do not* remove the other cups and put them on the ground. Loose cups are not only useless but also dangerous, for they have a way of hiding in the grass until someone steps on them. And unless the pin is attached, it will disappear instantly and forever.

- When you're finished and have no special reason to dismantle the whole course, always leave something jumpable. Maybe the next rider can use the fences just as they are, or will need only to adjust heights or distances. But if everything is left on the ground, or even worse, stacked in a pile, you are condemning the next rider to starting from scratch for no reason. Piling everything together is worst of all, since the rails or standards you want are invariably on the bottom of the pile. If you do intend to dismantle the course, still observe the pairs of standards rule—keep the pairs with the same cups and of the same height together—and keep rails of the same color together. This will facilitate things enormously for the next builder and is no more than common courtesy.

• Remember that leaving rails on the ground for any length of time kills the grass (if there is any) and eventually rots the rails. You can avoid this, when stacking rails, by placing one rail lengthwise, and then placing everything else with one end elevated on the lengthwise rail. Also remember always to leave an empty hole between adjacent cups, for if one cup sits directly on top of another, there is no way to insert a rail except endwise, and the rail so inserted cannot come down. (Even if you don't want to use a rail there, you will still have to move the cup before you can use it.)

• Many rails end up with a slight "set" or bow in one direction, and it is preferable always to turn the bow down. Perhaps there is some kind of optical illusion involved here, for rails that bow *up* are somehow very easy to knock down. (You have the right, incidentally, to ask jump crews in the show ring always to reset fences with the bow turned down, and should they have forgotten to do so in resetting a fence just before you go, you should call it to their attention.)

• Do not invariably build only ramps, or verticals with perfect ground lines a foot or two from the base of every fence. When you get to the average show, you will very rarely find that the course designer has obliged by building all of his fences the same way. Deprived of the ground line "crutch" to which you've accustomed them, many horses will proceed to go very badly. Instead, you should school over fences that are built just the way they'll be built in the show ring, or in an even harder form. Verticals should be strictly vertical, and not too fully filled out; oxers should be really square. If your horses can cope with this kind of fence at home, the beautifully dressed show ring fences will ride even better, while the rider who insists on building a steady diet of ramps at home often gets a disappointing result at the show.

In this regard I should mention that a show or competition is really an opportunity to display publicly how your horse is going, and if it's not going very well at home without using take-off rails everywhere, you don't have much to display. On average, if you can reproduce 80 percent of your best schooling form in actual competition, you're doing well. And those occasions when the public and the lights and the flowers inspire your horse to give 120 percent of its best are gifts from the gods. It's silly to show a horse that's going badly at home in hopes that the show ring atmosphere will make it improve. It hardly ever does.

Nine

COURSE
WALKING
AND
COMPETITIVE
STRATEGY

I hope I have convinced you, by now, that we make good jumps by getting to the right spot in the right way. The remaining question is: how can we arrange to do this most consistently?

In the Dark Ages, when I started showing jumpers, most riders did it all "off their eye" or "from the seat of the pants." You'd ride toward the fence in a collected canter until you were close enough to "see your stride." Then you'd take a couple of driving strides (or as the British used to say, "give it two kicks and a jerk") and jump the fence. Once on the other side you'd pull up and start all over again. It all sounds impossibly primitive today. But when you consider that courses then were mostly collections of single fences, with only an occasional spread fence or in-and-out, that time was never a factor and that we never got to walk the courses in advance, it made pretty good sense. Nor were the real "mechanics" of those days any slouches; I've seen horses jump *six-foot* single rails! And I myself once jumped off over four fences, twice around, with everything except the first fence sitting on top of six-foot wings; neither horse in the jump-off had a rail down! Of course, that was all before golfers measured out every distance to the inch, and baseball managers fed all their statistics into a computer. But even way back then there were a certain number of stride counters. I know, because I was one of them.

These days, if the riders didn't invariably get to walk the course before riding it, you could still make a case for letting the horse figure out the striding, though it would have to be a pretty smart horse. Modern course designers use subtle adjustments in the spacing of fences as a principal means of obtaining a desirable result (not too many horses in the jump-off, no basketball scores or disasters, a clear-cut victory for the winner, preferably with clean rounds). The riders are given the opportunity, during their inspection of the course, to spot the problems and figure out solutions to them. Obviously, riders in all of the jumping disciplines (hunters, equitation and Three-Day too) owe it to themselves and to their horses to become proficient in course walking and in solving distance problems. By knowing what's coming up next, they should be able to adjust the horse's stride during the approach so as to give it the best chance to negotiate the obstacle(s) cleanly. If you can do that all around the course, you will be consistently successful.

Some die-hards still insist that the horse knows best, but few of these have had much show ring success. "Well, a loose horse never falls," is one of their time-worn arguments. Not so. Any experienced horseman knows that he can tip over a horse in a loose school virtually at will. (Needless to add, if he ever does so, he deserves a long rest away from horses and some good psychiatric counseling.)

All right, then, what do you have to know in order to become a good course walker? First of all, you must know that the average horse's average galloping stride measures about twelve feet in length. This can be shortened to eight or nine feet without losing too much impulsion, and lengthened to fourteen or fifteen without becoming impossibly flat, depending on the individual horse. And you must know that the average stride takes the best part of a second (about .06) to perform. (The time required for the jump itself is more variable. Horses that are quick in the air don't take much more time over little fences than their stride requires, but horses that get very high and "hang in the air" seem to take forever.)

Naturally, your score in faults over the course will reflect the number of obstacles you met perfectly (or at least well enough to jump cleanly), while your elapsed time will reflect the number of strides you took and their speed. This will in turn reflect the line you took and the amount of checking you did.

There are many different course-walking techniques, some of them quite fastidious. The one I've always used is the simplest and quickest one I know that still gives you the information you require.

Before you set foot on the course, take a long look at the course diagram posted at the in-gate and read everything written on it. If you are showing a jumper, you will need to know the speed on which the Time Allowed is based, the placement of the start and finish markers, any compulsory turning points, whether or not there are any closed obstacles, and, equally important, the jump-off course, if any. You should already have checked the class conditions in the official prize list. (If any of the above terms is puzzling to you and you want to be a show jumper, I urge you to get a rule book and study it.)

Since your examination of the course plan has given you a general idea of the trace of the course, you now go to the start and pass through it on the line you will take to the first fence. Since you'll obviously have to jump the first fence "off your eye" it is not necessary to count strides to it, but you still need to give it a good look and start thinking of the line you'll want to take to the second fence. You should be especially interested in the depth of the cups and the weight of the rail, if a rail is the top element. How much of a bump will this first fence take? Usually course designers tend to "give" you the first fence, but not always, and it's important to be able to estimate how much liberty you might be able to take with any fence on the course, including the first one.

Having inspected the first fence from the take-off side, you move to the landing side and place yourself about where you think your horse is likely to land, say, six feet or so from what will be the highest point of its arc over the fence. You now start walking toward the second fence on the line you've chosen, taking strides you know (from actual measurement) are almost exactly three feet in length. (For short striders this will be quite a reach, but that doesn't matter as long as you know what it feels like, and can reproduce the feeling consistently.) Four walking strides equal one "average" galloping stride of your horse. The way to keep track of the horse's stride that I have always used is to count to myself, "ONE, two, three, four. TWO, two, three, four. THREE, two, three, etc. etc."

If you arrive at a good take-off spot for the second fence (as well as any of the fences that follow) on a count of four, you know that the distance will ride well if you simply do everything normally, and there's really no reason to concern yourself with the actual number of strides involved. Say to yourself, "fences one to two, come normally." Ordinarily, if any distance walks normally, or is very easy to make by going forward, that's the way I'll ride it, for I feel that if the course designer has given you a comfortable distance, it would be silly not to take it. In principle, *going* is always slightly safer than *checking*, because it takes less riding—and the less the intervention of the hand, the less likely it is that the horse will get "bent out of shape" in resisting.

With a normal distance it's also obvious that you automatically know what adjustment to make if your horse happens to jump the first fence *other* than normally. If you were slow or sticky over the first fence, you'll need to come on a bit to catch up with the distance; while if you happened to jump the first fence extra boldly with a big "stand back," you'll need to steady a little, or else "land and go" and leave out a stride.

Of course, even the perfect distance also affords two other options that you may prefer for some particular reason. You can add a stride, or even two, by checking as you land; and while I think it is making unnecessary problems for yourself if you do this as a matter of course (as some British riders still do), there may also be valid reasons for doing so. For example, your horse may be very "quick," and you want to make it wait; the next fence may be a difficult vertical that comes down very easily, and you want to ride it very carefully (it is dangerous to be too "nice" in jumping such fences); the next fence may be a very tight (short) combination, and you dare not jump in too far; or the next fence may set up a very sharp turn, and you want to be able to turn a bit in the air and not land too deeply.

The second option is choosing to leave out a stride (or even two) because none of the above factors prevails, and you want to be in an attacking mode for what follows; or because you are going against the clock and need to save that second or two.

Now, what about the situation in which you arrive at the next take-off spot not on a count of four, but on a count of two—exactly half a stride out? You know that you will meet the fence wrong unless you make some adjustment, but the adjustment you make will again depend upon your particular horse and the particular tactical situation. With a quick horse, you will ordinarily steady and make the extra stride unless you are going against the clock. (The virtue of quick horses is that they always want to get quicker, so you generally make them wait until time becomes a critical factor.) With the average or sluggish horse, you're often better off leaving out the stride, not only because it's easier, but because you need to encourage the horse to move forward more freely.

Whichever solution you choose to the half-stride problem, the place to execute it on horseback will be during the landing from the previous fence and during the first couple of strides thereafter. (This becomes truly critical if only a few strides are involved.) To make the extra stride,

you steady the horse a bit in the air and during the landing phase of the previous fence, and take a couple of
controlled strides; at this point you should begin to see a
good, normal stride for the next fence. If you are riding to
leave the half-stride out, you give your horse a lot of
freedom in the air, and sort of nudge it forward as it
lands, so that there is no constraint at all for the first
couple of strides after landing. You are not *looking* for a
distance; you *know* for sure that if you land and go, it will
be there.

These techniques are absolutely essential when the
distance problem is inside a combination, for if you allow
a normal landing and a normal landing stride to take
place and only then start to adjust, you are doomed. For
example, if there is a short two-stride distance between
two big oxers—say, thirty-two feet—you will have to try
to cheat your way in over the first oxer off a very steady
stride, restrain the landing stride as much as you dare
without killing your impulsion and then drive more or less
normally in your second stride. If you take a normal long
stride on landing over the first fence, you will have to
choke the take-off stride for the second fence, and may
never get to the far side of the second oxer if it has much
spread.

The most extreme example of this problem that I have
ever encountered was in the 1960 Olympic Games in Rome.
In the individual competition there was a nine-meter
(twenty-nine feet six inches) distance between the second
and third elements of the triple combination, which were
a triple bar to a big oxer. The distance from the first fence
(a wall) to the triple bar was short, so it was not possible
to attack very strongly; you had to chip in over the wall,
risk having the triple bar down behind in cheating over
the triple bar and then try to squeeze in two strides to the
oxer, since it was virtually impossible to jump it in one. (I
say "virtually," because Hans Günter Winkler's Halla did
it that way in the second round, and made it look not only
possible, but almost easy.) Nearly every horse in the competition had this fence down at least once, not even count-
ing falls and refusals.

This may all sound pretty complicated, but in practice

it is quite simple. One thing I never bother with is the actual number of strides—I do *not* count, "one, two, three, etc." as I ride to the next fence. It just makes an unnecessary complication. In memorizing courses, I use a trick musicians use to memorize a score, stressing the sequence of fences as well as the fences themselves, and I throw in the riding instructions to myself as I go. (If you think fence by fence, you may get stuck as to what comes next.) As I go through the fences one after another by number, I always visualize each particular fence. For example, I think to myself, "One to two; two to three; three to four, come steady; five to six; six to the triple, come strong, but steady over the oxer (the middle fence); seven to eight," etc., etc.

Let me reiterate, I visualize each fence as I say its number to myself, and just ride normally unless I tell myself something different. The advantage to this system is that as you land over fence three, you subconsciously say to yourself, "three to four, come steady" without even having to think about it. What you try to do by going over courses in this way is to store them in your memory so that the whole process becomes automatic. But you also reinforce it by visualizing the course diagram itself, and especially by studying the geometric pattern of the line. ("Up the near side, back down the diagonal, jump the fence in the end, circle back over the wall," etc., etc.)

In walking the course and memorizing it, I use five different kinds of riding instructions:

- If I say nothing to myself, it means, "Ride normally," taking about twelve-foot strides.
- If I say, "Come steady," it means, "Land and *don't* go; take shortish strides and jump the next fence out of hand."
- If I say, "Come strong," it means, "Land and go right to the next fence without checking, taking somewhat longer strides and looking to stand back at the next fence."
- If I say, "Override the distance," it means, "Land going and immediately drive at the next fence so that you not only leave out the stride, but also get close enough to the next fence to be able to steady your horse as it

leaves the ground." (This can be a very useful tactic against the clock if your horse can take a long stride, but not every horse can get there.)

• If I say, "Kill the stride," it means, "Make a fairly abrupt half-halt and start all over again." Sometimes you need to do this if the course designer has given you something really difficult, such as a nice "going" distance to a very tight combination. If you take the distance he has given you, you have no chance. You must either kill the stride or, with the right horse against the clock, override it so that you can still take a real pull at the horse as it jumps into the combination.

The last two instructions are quite exceptional, and even the second and third are not often called for over most "average" courses. I must confess that I enjoy distance problems, because I think they bring the best horses and riders to the top. I regret that only a handful of designers seem to enjoy inventing them, and those who do are sometimes criticized for it even though they are, in fact, the very best. Most course designers at ordinary shows (especially those who build hunter courses) routinely try to feed you nothing but good distances, presenting you with a problem only by mistake. For example, lines that are slightly downhill tend to ride tighter than they walk (and vice versa), and the designer sometimes may forget this. Riders as well as course designers tend to forget that a "good" distance is only good within its own particular context (its height, spread if any, types of fences and situation on the course).

Because I mistrust ideas such as: "twenty-five feet is a 'good' distance, whatever the circumstances," I prefer to walk distances from an estimated landing spot to an estimated take-off spot. Oh, sure, I sometimes also walk the "inside" distance, from the far rail of the first fence to the near rail of the second, just out of curiosity to see what the actual measurement is. But unless you are a course designer yourself, what counts is the way it will ride, not how long it measures, and the latter doesn't always give you the former.

For you purists, I will admit that my pragmatic method

involves a small fallacy: if you observe where horses actually take off, land and end their strides, you will note that their actual take-off and landing distances from the fence are rarely equal, and if they take two strides in a combination, the two strides are rarely of equal length. In practice, horses usually take off closer to the fence than we estimate they will, and land deeper; and the landing stride is usually longer than the last stride before their takeoff. But to adjust for all of this while walking distances is unnecessarily complicated and tells you nothing additional that you need to know. Walking twelve-foot strides and judging take-off and landing spots with your eye is still the best way to know what you have to do in riding a course.

Incidentally, an easy way to confirm your riding plan is to go back to the problem distance and walk it, not in twelve-foot strides, but in strides of the length you plan to take. You have a half-stride to make up, and you plan to add the stride? Go back to your landing spot, take three ten-foot strides, and then your normal twelves, and you will see exactly where that puts you and how it feels. Riding the same stride will give you exactly the same feeling: you land and wait for a couple of strides and then you proceed normally.

Making the Time Allowed

So far I have been talking primarily about jumping fences cleanly, but there is another way to make faults on a jumping course: by exceeding the Time Allowed. These time faults are not so much incurred as given away, for really good riders rarely get into time-fault problems, while average riders do it all the time. And this is a shame, because there is quite a simple way to avoid them.

Many of the important outdoor competitions—outdoor Nations' Cups, Grands Prix and the stadium jumping phase of the Three-Day Event—base their Time Allowed on four hundred meters per minute. This was no doubt quite practical in the "old days," when fences were smaller and lines more straightforward, but today's more complicated lines and more frequent turns mean that parts of the course simply cannot be ridden at such a speed, and there are not enough places where the time lost can be made up by galloping.

The only rational thing to do (as has been noted by surprisingly few riders) is to find some spot on the course where you can turn well inside the line the course measurer must walk, yet do so to a relatively easy fence or to one that you plan to ride very much in hand anyway. Often this will be a fence that you have to turn back to, with or without a turning point that the measurer will have walked around. If you can turn *inside* the point the measurer has gone around, fine. In any case, there's nothing to be gained and much time to be lost by landing over a fence and going farther and farther away from the next fence, to which you must eventually turn back. (A glance at the accompanying diagram will make this clear.) If you simply make one good turn at this point, and shorten your own line by twenty or thirty meters, you can then enjoy the luxury of riding the rest of the course normally (provided, of course, that you don't loiter), and still make the time.

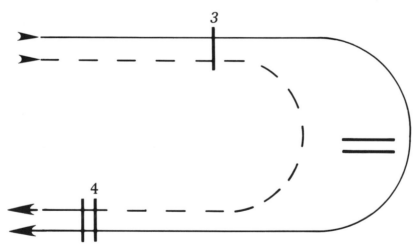

————Line the course designer and jury must measure

----------Line you should ride to make Time Allowed while taking minimum risk

Very occasionally you may have to find two turns of this sort, and you should do it if you have to. Anything is better than throwing away an important competition through a completely unnecessary time fault. (World Championships and Olympic gold medals have been lost in just this way!) Pick the safest fence to turn to, and make a good turn to it; then ride the rest of the course as you prefer to. It is especially important to remember this tactic after a refusal. If you can "save your time" and stay within three seconds of the Time Allowed, you will still beat all of the four-faulters, and this margin can make a tremendous difference in multiphase competitions such as the World Cup and World Championships.

• • •

Now let me offer a few words of tactical advice about particular types of competitions.

Ordinary Speed Classes (Time the first round, fault and out, Table C, etc.)

The basic key to being fast is simple: start in the tempo you want to end with, land and go to the next fence on the shortest possible line and don't check unless you have to when you get there. Bear in mind that slow clear rounds are useless in the average speed class—if you're lucky, you'll be beaten by only a dozen horses. So first, you've got to be faster. Then, if you're skillful and lucky enough to leave all the fences up, you'll win.

How do you leave everything up, going that fast? To be honest, mostly by having good horses. Much of the time you'll simply be riding a line, putting the fences in your horse's way and improvising ways to jump them when you get there. Of course, you have to help a bit; nobody jumps a lot of verticals cleanly going flat out, and you can't make a lot of "crest releases" and leave much of anything up. But wait until you're close to the next fence before checking, and even then check only if you're pretty certain you can't jump the fence unless you do. Landing and checking before looking for the next fence is just plain silly, unless the only reason you're in the class is to give a green horse a look at some low fences. And remember: since the fences are low, and many are built fairly solidly, you can usually take some liberty with most of them and still leave them up. So sacrifice a bit of precision and ask your horse to show its class by being brave and clever.

You should also realize that, when riding against the clock, if you go through the start faster than anyone else, ride a tight line and never check, you cannot be beaten. The safest place to take the maximum risk is often over the first fence or two, for they are usually built in such a way that you can jump them a bit too fast and get away with it; no course designer wants the first fence to come down very often. I borrowed this idea from the great Olympic skier Jean-Claude Killy, who observed that you should be emotionally prepared to attack the first two gates of a slalom course just as aggressively as the final two, since the first ones could usually take it better. This can sometimes give you the leeway to play it safe during the more difficult parts of the course. It's a clever concept, and it works in show jumping, too.

There will, of course, be circumstances in which winning is not "the only thing." For example, if you go late on an average horse in an ordinary kind of class, and some blazing clear rounds have already been posted, you may prudently decide to jump a slow clear, take nothing out of your horse, pick up your little ribbon and wait for a class that offers better odds. Where this obviously does not apply is in major competitions. If you have a chance to win a big title, you have to take a crack at it. In such circumstances, aiming at the middle of the standings isn't very satisfying even if you hit your objective.

Accuracy Classes (All AHSA Table 1 classes, Nations' Cups, jump-off qualifiers and classes in which a clear is the principal thing.)

In general, the key to all accuracy classes is to enter the ring on a horse that is prepared to try to jump clean, and to ride approaches that are as perfect as you can make them. Most of the time a horse that has jumped fifty fences outside in warming up will not only be warm, but will have begun to lose interest. Just as the racetrack is full of "morning glories" that run their best during their workouts, many show jumpers seem to leave their clear rounds outside in the collecting ring. I'd prefer to jump a maximum of only six to eight fences outside, and perhaps let my horse touch one of them just hard enough to know it's there, by being ridden a bit tight to it. (No wreck, please!)

Galloping into the ring to make your salute is a certain way of ensuring that the horse is awake and that it has some "revs." Before saluting, make a good halt to assert control, be sure to wait for the judge's signal and then make a good circle to the first fence. (Sitting in the judges' box, as I often do these days, I'm surprised at the number of horses that come into the ring half asleep or only half prepared; you can often guess how they're going to perform before they even jump a fence.)

From there on, concentrate on executing your riding plan, starting off at the right tempo for the whole course and trying to meet each fence exactly as you've planned. Your goal is to pull up at the end of the course with a clear round, having given your horse good preparation for the jump-off or the second round, and having taken relatively little out of it physically.

Jump-offs

Here your emphasis must be on a combination of speed tactics and accuracy tactics, depending on the size of the course—the bigger it is, the greater the accuracy required—and on the order in which you were drawn. (Who ever said that life was fair?) If you're going toward the end, or, even better, last, you'll know exactly what you have to do—whether you have only to jump a clear round, or can get by with an 80 percent "cut," or have to go flat out. So your tactics will pretty much be dictated by what's happened ahead of you. If you're going early with a good horse and you have a lot of good riders behind you, you must realize that a slow clear probably won't do you much good. (The only exception might be when the course designer seems embarrassed by having gotten too many clears, and overreacts by raising *everything* in the jump-off.) So you have to decide more or less whether to write off your chance of winning or go all out in a preemptive round and put so much pressure on the following riders that they have to take too many risks.

Again, the Killy tactic applies here; attack whatever there is on the course that can stand being attacked, and try to be very accurate over fences that are very difficult or come down very easily. Let me warn you against easing up on your horse too suddenly; I have seen fabulous rounds ruined by riders who tried to play the last fence too safe, and permitted the horse to let down when they would probably have jumped the fence cleanly if they'd only kept coming. (It's rather like the golfer who birdies his way to the lead, and then loses it when he starts playing for pars.)

Mickey Mouse Classes (I'm sorry, that's how I think of them.)

These include the Match Race, Jigsaws, Gamblers, Relays and the like.

They are supposed to be fun for the audience and fun for the riders, but I always found it hard to have fun while putting up ragged performances, which these class conditions tend to require. Good course designers can sometimes mitigate the down-side of Gamblers classes with brilliantly placed fences; but I generally preferred to get by in these classes and leave them to riders whose competitive urges were irresistibly aroused by them. Whatever you do, don't ruin your horses simply because the class conditions encourage you to do so.

Puissance Classes, Six-Bar and High Jump

These three kinds of classes all have something in common, though the last two are relatively rare these days: all are basically sheer tests of power and accuracy. They can be fun if you have the right horse for them, and you can win a much higher percentage of Puissance classes than any other if you happen to have the right horse. If you don't—and a legitimate seven-foot-plus horse is a minimal requirement for top-class competition these days— you should watch the class from the stands.

If you are lucky enough to have a real Puissance horse, you have to find out by experimentation what its most natural style of jumping a big fence is, and then try to do that very consistently. Many horses, especially the more powerful type, seem to do best by being more or less compressed against the wall in their last stride, and jumping right from the base. This kind of horse seems to feel that it will be unable to "tip" or bascule if it stands back too far. Others (like Bold Minstrel, which I used to ride) are more comfortable standing back a bit further and making more of a spring than a push. But you have to determine *the horse's* preference.

If the wall is constructed to come down fairly easily, it's a good idea to ride at it from a slight angle, since the blocks will not come down quite so readily if they are hit on the bias, as it were. The principal problem in riding down to a single big fence will always be overeagerness and anticipation, so take plenty of time and use plenty of room; be deliberate, confident and accurate. Incidentally, with a fairly good horse (which is the only kind you should show in such competitions) I'd take my chances rather than ask it to hit the optional warm-up fence before every round. Even if the horse hits it, it usually seems to be more counterproductive than useful, and I wouldn't shed a tear if the FEI did away with it altogether.

Six-Bar classes have the advantage of not getting quite so big, and it's really just a question of finding the right tempo, so that your speed perfectly matches the two-stride spacing of the fences. For many long-striding horses, the mandatory distance of "about eleven meters"—(thirty-six feet)—can be a bit tight when the fences get high. One of the most unusual things I ever saw in a six-bar competition occurred at the 1974 World Championships at La Baule, France. There the Six-Bar was specified to be a two jump-off class, the second against the clock. (This was probably done to save the horses, though it's really a contradiction in terms.) Frank Chapot won the class with San Lucas by leaving out a stride to the last fence and taking a whole second off the previous best time. Walk that off some time, and you'll realize what a superhorse San Lucas was!

Ten

DEALING
WITH
PROBLEM
TEMPERAMENTS

*R*iding instruction, written and otherwise, usually seems to be based on the assumption that the rider is dealing with an "average" horse—an animal that is reasonably calm, willing and receptive to the rider's aids (correctly applied). In real life, however, this average horse seems as much a statistical fallacy as the average man, for the individuals we have to work with invariably fall well one side or the other of "normal," usually inclining toward more excitability or more laziness than we would ideally prefer. Indeed, horses exhibit almost as wide a range of personalities as do people, and the simple, compliant, "average" horse seems to be in the distinct minority.

The fact that a horse may have a somewhat difficult temperament does not mean that it cannot be of the very highest class. Show jumping annals are replete with marvelous examples of both basic types, even in their extreme form. The hotter type includes such matchless superstars as Halla, Posillipo, Snowbound, Touch of Class and Jappeloup (to name only Olympic gold medalists), all of them highly strung, gymnastic and explosive, capable of running all day on nervous energy alone. At the opposite end of the spectrum are such heavier types as Meteor, The Rock, Fire, Aramis and The Natural, more stolid horses that may tire if they have to carry their weight too far, but with the compensating virtues of great strength and substance, and far less temperamental inflammability.

Common though these basic types of equine personality are, the means of dealing with them are often more or less ignored by teachers, who imply that if what you're doing doesn't work, you must be doing it wrong. In fact, however, if you persist in treating problem temperaments just as you do ordinary ones, you are *doomed*. Hot horses and duller ones need to be treated differently right from the beginning, even before you get on their backs. In fact, much of the problem of dealing with difficult temperaments isn't really a riding matter at all—it's something that must first be approached on the level of overall stable management.

Until recently, certain trainers, while agreeing with this last statement, would automatically interpret it to mean that you must cope with difficult temperaments by finding the right level of tranquilizer or stimulant for the individual case. More comprehensive drug testing, both at home and abroad, has done much to discourage this attitude, but it is still advisable to get a drug test on any horse you are thinking of buying—or even better, a trial in your own barn if the dealer will agree. Unfortunately, some people *still* consider drugs the ultimate labor-saving device.

What can you do, short of resorting to drugs? A lot. The first rule with hot horses is simple: *never fight the oats*. Oats tend to be temperamentally intoxicating (the English expression "feeling your oats" is synonymous with rambunctious behavior), and keen horses usually do much better on some combination of bran, pellets, sweet feed and hay. Sluggish horses, on the other hand, usually tend to be fat as well as lazy, and the first rule with them is equally simple: *get them fit, and keep them thin.*

Buyers purchasing horses from smart horsemen should remember how much flesh was on the horse when they liked it well enough to buy it. I've seen slightly undernourished horses turn into real terrors when they got fattened up, and I've seen other reasonably athletic-looking horses get so fat overnight that they couldn't get out of their own way. On average, however, and notwithstanding today's show ring taste for overly fat horses, most temperaments benefit from not standing too long at the feed trough.

The next set of useful adjuncts in dealing with problem temperaments is activity *not* under saddle—that is, turnout, longeing and time on a mechanical "hot-walker." (A hot-walker is a sort of electrically driven carousel to which horses can be attached, much in favor at American racetracks for cooling horses out.) The latter also has great value for horses recovering from leg injuries, while its inexorability can wear down even a rogue. It works equally well in taking an edge off a hot horse and keeping weight off a fat one.

Some sort of daily work routine that keeps a hot horse from "getting above himself" is essential, and in this regard long turnouts in a paddock small enough to discourage running can be very helpful. (In fact, where climate and bugs permit, I've known horses to improve dramatically by being turned out all night.) Under most circumstances, however, longeing is likely to be safer and more practical, and has the added advantage of educational value. The time it takes before you mount is more than made up by making your time in the saddle more productive.

What other steps can you take from the ground, so to speak? It is important to have a hot, fresh horse bitted in a way that affords sufficient control, although very severe bits are usually counterproductive. Martingales and draw reins are worth their weight in gold when a cold March wind gets under your horses' tails, and the fact that you can slip a finger under the martingale yoke in emergencies has kept many a rider from dismounting involuntarily. Snap-in draw reins and martingales are especially handy to add, subtract or exchange as needed. I don't think that many horses benefit from a whole session in draw reins, however; since you won't be allowed to use them in competition, you have to practice doing without them, too.

Essential tools in dealing with the more sluggish type of horse are spurs and a whip capable of attracting its attention. You are trying to make the horse more sensitive to the aids, and it is hard to do delicate surgery with a dull knife! No strong horse should ever have its mouth go numb from the unremitting pressure of a clumsy mouthpiece on its bars, and no lazy horse should have sides that are black and blue under the hair, or spots worn hairless by a dull spur. A tiny prick by a sharp spur or a quick "pay attention!" with a dressage whip are far more effective, and therefore, far more humane.

Once in the saddle, your goal with either kind of temperament will be to ride the horse from behind and to get it to perform in good mental and physical equilibrium: "calm, straight and forward." To accomplish this, you must teach both kinds of horses to accept your drive and express it in a good way, which will mean making the hot horse less "hair-trigger" and the sluggish horse quicker and more responsive. You cannot do either unless you sit in the middle of the horse and put it on the bit.

The biggest problem with hot horses, of course, is getting them to accept your driving aids, though the amount of leg and back they can take will never be very much. (When I first heard this idea, I asked myself, "Why should I want to *drive* at them when I can't hold one side of them?" Eventually I realized that that's the whole point.) Leg and back aids should at first be applied very gently and very discreetly; a brusque insistence to "come through" *now* is very rarely rewarded by a really difficult horse.

In general, hot horses need you to be a little late or a little slow in all of your responses; anticipation on your part is the worst thing, because anticipation is already a major part of their problem. In everything you do, you must only elicit the movement, and then wait to accompany it as it develops, in a very soft, slow-motion sort of way. With ordinary horses you must be careful about slowing down the tempo of the collected gaits too much; the feeling should be lively for the short strides and slower for the longer ones, to give them time to express themselves. But with quick horses, you must always work to slow down the tempo, for it will always tend to be too fast.

The sluggish horse will always want to slow the tempo down, and must be kept in front of your seat at all times, for if it can tip your shoulders forward you will have no influence at all. Instead, you must stay behind the horse's motion so that you can demand an increasingly lively tempo and a quicker and quicker response to your aids, creating the illusion of a quicker, livelier horse. Above all, you don't want to make so few demands, nor make them so tentatively, that the horse can simply plod along, bored to death.

A hot horse or a very fresh horse is best started off on a relatively small circle at a strong working trot. The fatal situation with a horse that's pulling and eager to go is to let it "handcuff" you, leaning equally on both reins, drawing your shoulders forward so that your influence is weakened. You must resist the horse's eagerness to scramble forward by turning, and you must resist its efforts to pull your shoulders forward by pushing forward with your pelvis until, bit by bit, you find it possible to ask the horse to lengthen its stride instead of always restricting it. Of course, at the beginning, you will often "lose it" and have to go back to the smaller circle, but by straightening your line for a few strides at a time you should eventually be able to preserve rhythm and shape and length of stride even when you push your horse forward quite aggressively.

Circling is also the answer to the hot horse that refuses to walk, and "jigs" instead. It takes a circle so small that the horse has no choice but to walk (ten or twelve feet in diameter is about right) and endless patience. But eventually you can convince every horse that if it takes a jigging step, it's going to spend five minutes on a tiny circle in consequence, and no amount of diplomacy can accomplish as much as positively.

Through all of this you must keep an eye on the horse's temperamental barometer, for what you are trying to do with a truly difficult horse is to create a little island of compliance in the midst of its ocean of resistance, and then gradually to enlarge it. You cannot achieve this if you are always picking at flaws and never rewarding, so you must sometimes "split the difference" and praise only a small improvement, or temporarily abandon an exercise that is fraught with anxiety for the horse and let it do something that it does well. Often this is just a question of pushing the horse forward, or giving it a pat and a moment or two on a loose rein. Within the daily work session you have to avoid simply making the horse angrier and angrier or hotter and hotter until it blows its top. So when you see warning signs that you're putting too much pressure on a hot temperament, you should back off a bit, and then start again when the horse is not quite so close to the boiling point. As your horse really starts to relax and is no longer so much "on the muscle," you can ask for a wider variety of movements: a little shoulder-in, a little collection, a little half-pass—thereby helping the horse find its proper balance and refine its response to your aids.

While much of the above advice is also valid for a sluggish horse, your principal problem in this case is the horse's willingness to rest its head on your hands, and gradually to ignore the action of your leg even though you push it halfway through the horse's rib cage. The horse is hoping that you'll take over more and more of the work, and if it succeeds, you'll end up providing all of the impulsion and holding the horse up, as well. Your solution is to explain with unmistakable clarity how you expect the horse to respond to your aids, and you do this by starting with light aids and escalating them very rapidly. For example: at the halt, you squeeze your calves very gently, and the horse ignores it. A little more, and it ignores that. Then you really belt the horse with your heel, saying, in effect, "Listen to my leg!" You squeeze gently again, and this time the horse responds by moving forward. Pat it and push forward more freely. You will have to repeat this sequence many times, always returning to the lightest indication. Whatever you do, you must adamantly refuse simply to use more and more leg; life is too short for that! Use a strong leg only as a correction, not as an aid, and *teach* your horse to respond sensitively to normal aids.

These exercises will have an automatic beneficial effect on the horse's jumping performance because the better your horse goes on the flat, the more ridable it will be over fences. Once the horse has settled well on the flat, whether on the longe or under saddle, you can proceed to work over cavalletti or rails on the ground at all gaits as well as over small fences jumped at the trot and the canter.

Though cavalletti and gymnastics are equally valuable for both types of temperaments, you should not expect them to serve as a substitute for good flat work. Cavalletti by themselves rarely help to slow the hot horse down, improve its impulsion or stabilize its mental attitude, but only test whether the horse is ready to tackle this new kind of challenge. For the hot horse, making approaches and then circling if it starts to hurry is not only the immediate remedy, but long-range therapy as well. Horses with excitable temperaments usually have a tendency to "get quick" for their whole lives, and you'll probably have to continue making some circles with them after every class and, especially, after every round jumped against the clock.

Both types of difficult temperaments need the reward of being ridden forward on a loose rein just as much as other horses do. This is, in fact, a key test for the hot horse, for until you can drop the reins without having it pick up speed, you cannot delude yourself that you are starting to find the solution. Sluggish horses need less time on loose reins than hot ones, since they often use them as an excuse to slow down and go back to sleep; even so, they need that occasional reward. Continuous concentration seems so hard for them! The main thing is to keep their "revs" up, even on a loose rein.

Predictably, warming up these two kinds of temperaments before a competition is also quite different. Some riders seem to think a hot horse needs to be worn down prior to the competition, but quite the opposite is true: the hot horse is "revved up" even standing still, and too many fences may wind it up too much. A fence or two is often quite enough for a high-strung horse. A sluggish horse, on the other hand, really *needs* a decent warm-up in order to get the engine going, although too many warm-up fences can cause it to lose interest. The tendency these days, it seems to me, is to overdo warming up with both types of horses. After twenty or thirty fences, any horse can be forgiven for losing some of its desire to jump fences cleanly.

Perhaps the most frustrating of all the difficult temperaments, and a surprisingly dangerous one too, is the timid or chickenhearted horse. Horses that are upset by any new sight or sound and have no faith in their ability get themselves into all sorts of impossible predicaments. Because they freeze and back off in tight spots instead of "taking a full swing," they can give you the worst kinds of falls. I have ridden some really talented horses of this temperament, and expended quantities of patience and tender, loving care on them, but my final conclusion is that the only thing that helps materially is a mild tranquilizing drug. Since these are strictly forbidden in competition, the best thing to do with a genuine shrinking violet is to find a career for it as a hack. (They make just as heartbreaking dressage horses as they do jumpers, since every new set of letters and every flower pot is potentially intimidating.)

So far our discussion of difficult horses has not extended to true rogues, though many of the techniques mentioned for hot horses are also applicable to pathological problem horses—the genuinely naughty, spoiled or dangerous ones. With them, the first rule is to pick your battlefield, and to pick a safe one. Never try to get to the bottom of a truly difficult horse in a place that gives it the advantage. Instead, choose an enclosed ring, free of distractions, trees and bushes, and with good, safe footing. Open fields, hard roads and uninvited company are highly dangerous if you're on a horse that may rear, wheel, run away or buck hard. The only answer to such vices is to ride forward and keep the horse's head up, and to ride well "behind the motion." Don't worry if you look a little "cowboy" until the horse smooths out a bit; just remember that very few riders ever fall off backward, and the old-fashioned "safety" seat is just the thing for such emergency situations.

With the rearer, the key thing to remember is to turn, which makes the horse put its feet back on the ground. (It is not a bad idea to put one arm under its neck, to ensure that you don't pull it over backward, while you turn with the opposite rein.) Should a horse really run away with you, the answer is also to turn, taking one rein in both hands and putting your feet "on the dashboard" if need be, until you can make a small enough circle to be able to reestablish control.

The best thing to do with a rank or "nappy" horse that doesn't want to go forward, is to make it *go somewhere*—in a different direction, or even backward—and then to draw it gradually back toward the direction in which you want to go. The horse that shies determinedly at something should be bent the opposite way (i.e., with its head turned away from the offending object) and ridden past it in a shoulder-in. If the horse is genuinely scared instead of merely resistant, it's sometimes better to get off and lead it past, through or over the frightening place. After several repetitions of this you can usually get back on and negotiate the awkward place mounted, with far less trouble than you would have experienced if you adamantly refused to meet the horse halfway. Panic is much harder to deal with than apprehension!

My experience with *true* rogues is not all that extensive, thank heavens, though the few I've handled afforded some heart-stopping moments. My guess is that 75 percent of the horses that appear to be rogues are really only badly scared or spoiled, and thus have a real chance of being reformed by someone who knows what he's doing. Even so, I've also seen a few horses that were simply and immutably *bad news*, perhaps due to genetic defects, and I urge you to let someone else sort these out the minute you so identify them.

The old-fashioned horse breakers of the nineteenth century created a fascinating literature about various extreme measures which have worked in the right hands. Devices such as the War Bridle (which exerts nerve pressure on the poll) and the Running-W (which enables you to pull the horse's legs out from under him at will) are still used skillfully and successfully in many parts of the world, and not just on difficult horses. At this point in my life, however, I'm quite content to leave such measures and the horses that need them to the experts and the history books.

Eleven

BITS AND BITTING

*P*roperly speaking, bits should never be discussed except in conjunction with a discussion of the action of the hand in consort with the other aids. For while horses have definite opinions about bits, and have a right to them (after all, it's *their* mouth), it's not so much because the horse "likes" a certain bit, but that it finds the action of the rider's hand more acceptable, or more comprehensible, through the medium of that particular bit. Even so, bits and bitting have fascinated horsemen all the way back to the earliest equestrian literature.

Different bits have existed for millennia. The ancient

Greeks, Romans and Assyrians invented some of the patterns we still use today. Xenophon, writing in about 365 B.C., urged riders to own at least two bits—a mild one, and a harsher one to make the horse appreciate the mild one. There is a good measure of common sense in this (as there is in much of Xenophon's advice), although modern riders prefer to own quite a few in-between bits as well. Indeed, many of them possess (as I do) quite extensive bit collections, even though they rely most often on a few old favorites.

Books and manuscripts on riding from the sixteenth century generally included extensive illustrated catalogues of bits, some patterns being so fanciful that one wonders if they ever actually existed except on paper. The Duke of Newcastle dismissed all this a century later with the tart observation that if the art of riding were simply a matter of finding the right bit, then bit makers would be the best horsemen. (He went on to note that the great Pignatelli used only simple bits, and told those who expressed amazement at what he could accomplish with them that "it was only their ignorance that made them wonder at his art.")

Bitting is complicated by the fact that the bit must suit not only a particular horse, but also a particular rider and the task at hand. As one who hates to be "taken," I rank practical control as the primary consideration, taking into account the level of training, strength and temperaments of both horse and rider. In addition, the bit must fit and be adjusted properly, and also please the rider's aesthetic sense. Fit is mostly a question of the width and thickness of the mouthpiece in relation to the size of the horse's mouth; I prefer an adjustment that leaves at least two wrinkles in the corners of the horse's mouth (one and one half is the minimum). Some might consider this high, but for me, bits that hang too low are even worse than a higher adjustment, for they invite the horse to put its tongue over the bit, a habit that can prove very difficult to correct.

Aesthetics are more personal; some riders even seem to feel that a little rust adds character to a bit! For me, the critical factor is the size and thickness of the ring(s) in relation to the size of the horse's head. Heavy, small rings on a big head make it look plain, while generous, thinner rings (like those of the typical English racing snaffle) make the head look smaller and more refined. All in all, bits and bridles should be in proportion to the horse that's wearing them.

Prior to World War II, England produced a huge range of different bit patterns, first in hand-forged steel that had to be burnished, later in plated or stainless metal. High manufacturing costs eventually curtailed the variety of patterns from English sources, but in recent years the Korean and German bit makers have more than made up for it. Today, in addition to a plethora of copper-mouthed bits (which I have never found to make much difference) there are even bits with mouthpieces made of "space age" plastics, some with a choice of impregnated flavors (carrot, apple) that horses seem to like very much.

The basic forms of snaffle, pelham and full bridle (bit and bridoon) have been around for centuries, and each has its adherents and detractors. The most common bit today (as in Xenophon's time) remains the jointed snaffle, and some maintain that what you cannot accomplish with a snaffle is not worth accomplishing. On the other hand, I've heard it remarked disdainfully that "snaffle bits are for people with snaffle hands." This is not necessarily a contradiction, but suggests that riders who use only snaffle bridle are likely to be (like anglers who use only a single fly pattern in various sizes) either very expert or very novice.

I find very thick mouthpieces clumsy, and dislike small rings that can be pulled through the horse's mouth too easily in emergencies. Full-cheek snaffles preclude this problem, but should ordinarily be used with a keeper that fixes the bit to the cheek-piece, preventing the joint from dropping too low in the horse's mouth. I'm partial to egg-butt snaffles, if the ring is large enough and the mouthpiece of a good width, but these are hard to find.

I am also partial to pelham bits, notwithstanding the fact that many authorities have condemned them for their alleged lack of a "pure" snaffle effect. Many horses (who never bother to read the authorities anyway) go well in them, benefiting from the mild curb effect without having to cope with a whole mouthful of metal. (Snowbound was one of these.) I am not so fond of Kimberwickes, for with them the degree of curb effect is not under the rider's control, but I remember that many of Francisco "Paco" Goyoaga's horses went brilliantly in them, and a new "elevator" variation on the same theme is the height of fashion in Europe as I write.

An advantage of pelhams and other straight-mouthed (unjointed) bits is the fact that they are available with a variety of ports, which have helped an even greater variety of wandering tongues. Of course, it is rightly said that the only true solution for the horse that puts its tongue over the bit lies in equestrian tact, but this is not easy to demonstrate in practice. The most helpful bitting solution I have observed was the one that Frank Chapot used with San Lucas: an angled port through which the horse can insert its tongue. These are now available from Korea both as (unjointed) snaffles and pelhams.

You don't see many full (double) bridles these days except in the dressage area, but the bit and bridoon combination remains the most subtle and versatile of all for the well-trained horse. (It should never, of course, be used on spoiled or insensitive horses simply for its potential severity.) The instant availability of any mixture of curb and snaffle effects can accomplish wonders in trained hands, though most riders and horses will do better with the snaffle or pelham until their training is quite advanced. Earlier remarks as to fit and aesthetics apply here, too. It is common to see the snaffles of full bridles adjusted too low, and it is hard to find a beautiful (that is, flattering) set; usually the bridoon rings are too small, the shanks of the curb unnecessarily long and the mouthpiece unnecessarily thick.

As long as I've been around horses, bitless bridles (hackamores) and the various forms of gags have been cyclically in and out of fashion, depending on whether some particular star rider was using them at the time. In recent years the example of Eddie Macken's Boomerang and Paul Schockemöhle's Deister has encouraged many riders to try the hackamore, in case it might prove one of the secrets of their outstanding success. (It's never quite that simple.) Currently, however, the hackamore may be going back into eclipse, although it remains a useful training aid for horses whose mouths have been badly spoiled or injured. Gags, on the other hand, have returned to favor, perhaps due to the success of the 1984 Olympic gold and silver medalists in show jumping, Joe Fargis and Conrad Homfeld, who used them with Touch of Class and Abdullah. Though gags may seem severe, one is surprised to find from the saddle that many horses accept them quite readily. They're effective insurance against being "taken" down to big fences faster than you want to go, especially cross country, as many eventers have come to appreciate.

Many different forms of noseband can modify or enhance the action of the bit. The figure-eight noseband was preferred by the 1948 Olympic champion, General Humberto Mariles, as it is by current stars such as Joe Fargis and Michael Matz; while a regular dropped noseband (or its "flash" variation), is still the commonest accessory in many parts of the world. Somehow my suspicion persists, however, that it's hard for a horse to be happy if it can't open its mouth. So these days (when I can afford to be less in a hurry than I used to be) I prefer an ordinary cavesson to all else, buckled not too tightly to prevent the horse from yielding its jaw, and adjusted two fingers below the cheekbone. (Cavessons pulled right up against the cheekbone make the nose look too long in relation to the rest of the face, and are almost as unattractive as the sagging browbands so often seen today.)

The other principal adjuncts to bitting are various forms of martingales, and draw reins. The latter can be extremely useful in retraining spoiled horses and at certain stages of training, as we have seen; but when they are used only to obtain a mechanical advantage, as is often the case, they can do a lot of harm as well. Draw reins will never be a substitute for educated hands.

It has always surprised me that the FEI rule prohibiting standing martingales has survived so long, for it is a piece of tack that is impossible to abuse and is routinely employed by many good horsemen. The prohibition came about, I suspect, because a well-known rider started using

a whole collection of tack on a certain difficult horse—
both running and standing martingales, with cavessons to
match. It might have been better to outlaw the use of two
martingales at the same time, because there's nothing
cruel about a standing martingale *per se*, and it can be
indispensable in retraining spoiled horses. (If it must be
outlawed, I'd rather see it disappear from the much-praised
Equitation Division in the United States, where its ubiqui-
tous presence has created generations of riders who are
totally incapable of influencing the horse's head carriage
with their hands.)

As for the running martingale, I would never ride in a
show jumping competition without one, unless there were
a specific bonus for doing so. It should be adjusted so that
it comes into action only when the horse raises its mouth
higher than its withers, and not so that the rein is always
pulled down, as if by a pulley, even when the horse's head
is in the right place. It is very common in the United
States these days to see running martingales adjusted
very long—so long, indeed, that the horse can hold its
head horizontally before the martingale comes into play—
and then the martingale becomes simply a necklace. (Its
only use then is to prevent both reins from getting on one
side of the horse's neck after a bad slip or near fall.)

Riding in competition without a properly adjusted running martingale thus seems to me sheer vanity. (If you
really want to show off, you might try an Irish martingale,
which is simply two rings connected by ten inches or so
of leather. The purpose of this device is to prevent the
horse from flipping both reins onto one side of its neck,
and there is no way in which the horse could put its leg
through it, as has been alleged to happen with very loose
running martingales.)

A well-trained horse won't normally bring the martingale into play very often during a round; but when one's
efforts to shorten stride are being resisted and the biggest fence on the course looms, that precious "nickel's
worth" of restraint can spell the difference between a
clear round and a wreck. I often ride at home with no
martingales at all, so that there is one less piece of tack to
clean; but when the money or the medals are on the line, I

urge you to take every legal advantage you can. And I'd guess that a properly adjusted martingale can save the average horse and rider about one knockdown out of four. Aside from the bit itself, no other single piece of equipment can make that much difference.

In the end, the horse itself will always be the final arbiter as to what is right and what is wrong about bits and bitting. I have long believed that if the horse can't finally accept what you're doing, it isn't any good: experience suggests that the horse will always ultimately reject solutions that have been imposed by force. What is more, its rejection will usually express itself at the most inopportune moment—just as you start your piaffe at X, or head for the biggest fence on the course. In riding, as in much else, less is often more; and since the horse will have the last word in any case, we must try to ensure, through skill, tact and moderation, that this last word is "yes."

---------------- *Twelve* ----------------

EVALUATING
THE
JUMPER

O nce you learn to ride jumpers, the problem is to find them—especially if your ambition is to ride over big fences and win Grands Prix. Though all horses are able to jump, as are cows and zebra, it must be admitted that the horse is a much less natural jumper than members of the cat and deer families. (Still, the horse that can carry a rider over a seven-foot wall will bring the crowd to its feet, while we pay scant attention to the family cat as it effortlessly leaps four or five times its own height onto the kitchen counter.)

"What do you look for in a jumper?" "What distinguishes a great horse from a very good one?" "What was the best

horse you ever rode?" These questions and similar ones
are probably asked more often of show riders than any
others, and we all develop ways of answering (or not
answering) them with shorter replies than they deserve.
(Necessarily so, for they are really hard questions to answer, requiring a lot of thought and a lot of explanation.)
My usual answers to these particular questions are (a) that
I look for the desire and ability to jump big fences cleanly
and in good form; (b) that the great horse produces its
best performance more often and over a longer period of
time; and (c) that if my life depended on jumping just one
more clear round over a big course, I'd like to be sitting
on Snowbound at his best. Often I add that show jumping
is no different from any other sport: outstanding performance depends on a combination of physical equipment,
talent and temperament, any one of which, if extraordinary enough, can largely compensate for fairly ordinary
attributes elsewhere.

As I write, Grand Prix or Olympic jumpers bring six
or even seven figures in the open market, which is absolutely mind-boggling to me; and even the higher class of
amateur hunter or jumper and the proven equitation horse
are worth a lot of money. At the other end of the scale are
backyard hunters and jumpers that hardly expect to travel
out of the state, much less abroad, but that provide their
riders with a lot of pleasure and experience, and can be
just as interesting to develop to their full potential as
some world-beater. While the matter of degree may vary,
these horses, too, must be evaluated according to the
same criteria: physical equipment, talent and temperament.

Let's examine these three factors in more detail. The
physical component can be broken down into structure,
natural movement and soundness, with *practical* soundness the indispensable ingredient. (If true greatness pre-
supposes a long career, no fundamentally unsound horse
ever gets to show more than brilliant promise.) Soundness and structure are of course related, for the better the
structure the sounder, on average, the horse. But practical
or "working" soundness is not quite the same thing as
ideal veterinary soundness, even though the latter would
be everyone's preferred starting point. In practice, the

jumper and the working hunter can learn to live with a lot of problems, and more than once I've seen horses struggle to pass the vet check and then prove to be consistent winners. Indeed, I can think of quite a few outstanding horses, with long careers, too, who *never* passed a veterinary examination. Even so, you'd surely better know what you're doing before you buy a horse against your vet's advice, and buying one without vetting it at all is *asking* for trouble.

Soundness of wind is a critical point for the show hunter, because many judges are absolutely ruthless if they suspect that a horse "makes a noise," even a very discreet one. With the jumper this is less important, provided that the horse does not blow your hat off, and has no trouble getting enough air into its lungs to carry it around a long course. (Indeed, many outstanding show jumpers were once hunters that became a bit "touched in the wind," and had to find another way to earn a living.) In any case, you want to know exactly what's there, and so should have a careful laryngyscopic examination done whenever you consider buying a horse, or suspect that something may be wrong with one you own. A lot can be accomplished surgically these days to help breathing problems, even though the cure may not always work out perfectly cosmetically.

Many thoughtful observers have tried to reduce the structural evaluation of jumping horses to a matter of angles, ratios and measurements, and the generalizations that result are quite valid: *on average* the horse with a nice, sloping shoulder, good pastern angulation, a knee that is over, if anything, rather than back, and a fairly straight hind leg is more likely to jump well than a horse less favorably endowed, even aside from questions of soundness. A big, healthy foot is especially important ("no foot, no horse"), and a decent length of front, with a neck put on properly and not "upside down," simplifies many riding problems. I also think that the horse with a shortish back is more likely to come off the ground all at once, rather than in sections. Having said all of this, however, I concede that there's a big difference between horses that look the part, and those that can do the job. The real source of an Olympic champion's excellence lies too deep to be revealed by a tape measure or a protractor.

Structure and movement are of course related, as are length of stride and basic jumping mechanism. And finally we must consider the matter of size and its frequent corollary, strength. I think we must accept the general proposition that, all else being equal, "a good big one is better than a good little one"—at least until awkwardness becomes a limiting factor. But there are certainly many fascinating exceptions, and it is easy to name dozens of horses under sixteen and even fifteen hands high that would be a match for anyone. The individual gold and silver medal winners at the 1988 Seoul Olympics, Jappeloup and Gem Twist, were both an inch or two shy of making sixteen hands, while the fabulous little Stroller, which won the silver medal in Mexico City, didn't even make fifteen hands. So size is not really critical unless there is a question of weight-carrying ability for the particular rider involved.

In earlier years, the European equestrian annual *L'Année Hippique* used to run a double-page spread of "conformation shots" of the leading international jumpers of the day. These were (and are) fascinating to study, but if there were inviolable structural common denominators among the models, I failed to detect them. Many horses that were brilliant over the course were very ordinary individuals standing still, and for every ravishing model that could really jump, there were half a dozen plainer horses that jumped even better.

The horse's natural movement on the flat is obviously related to its structure standing still, but you still have to watch them move before you can know how much rhythm they have, how straight they move and how much knee they have in their movement. In a jumper, many good horsemen prefer a bit of knee action in the trot and canter, feeling that the horse who bends its knee in moving on the flat will also do so more naturally over fences. (In fact, in the "old days," when most fences were vertical, a bit of hackney blood in the jumper was favored by many.) There may well be an element of truth in the converse, for quite a few of the Thoroughbreds with low, "daisy-cutting" actions are tempted simply to take long strides over fences instead of really jumping them. But again, there are many exceptions.

The real key ingredient is probably the elasticity of the horse's stride—its ability to shorten and (especially) lengthen stride. Long distances between spread fences in combination really *demand* the ability to take a long stride. Short-striding horses learn to land deeper into long combinations and take off farther away, but *extra-long* distances require the ability to take a long stride as well. Of course, the horse's capacity both to lengthen and to shorten stride must be developed through schooling, but it certainly helps if the horse has good natural balance in addition to its physical gifts. Some German-bred horses seem born with the instinct to make a little half-stride skip instead of shortening the stride, and this can be a useful skill in certain tricky situations.

Another variety of factors can be considered under the general heading of "talent." Pure jumping ability—the ability to get off the ground easily, whether through sheer power or gymnastic spring—is obviously the cardinal virtue in a jumper, and the more of it there is, the less critical is jumping technique *per se*. I have no doubt that the "knack" of jumping is usually inherited, for in the get of prepotent jumping stallions (as well as certain mares) a very high percentage of foals seem to come from the womb knowing how to jump.

Ideally the good jumper should be very free in its shoulders, so that in extension it can put its knees both very high and very forward, right up under its chin, while behind it should be able both to bend its hocks and pasterns and flip (bascule) its quarters, so that in the air its hooves are hardly lower than its stifle. However, horses that get high enough over their fences need not be all that immaculate about the way they bend their knees and hocks. Indeed, some horses that show a perfect technique over small fences do so because such fences are important fences to them, and quickly run out of scope as the fences become bigger. (Some genuine superhorses don't look like much over four-foot fences because they can virtually step over them without trying.) It is always wise to note where the horse's body is in relation to the fence, and if the body is high enough, the fact that the legs may hang a bit is not all that serious, except in hunter classes, when a good jumping style is of primary importance.

I find it a very positive sign for horses to make extravagant jumps when a fence looks a little funny to them, when they are in trouble and, sometimes, just because it's so easy for them to do it. Horses that choke up under the same circumstances don't jump very many clear rounds, though they may jump a lot of four-faulters. (When a tight spot rather than a probable wreck is imminent, riders must guard against becoming too cautious themselves and avoid "stiffing" the horse just as it is making its maximum effort. To see riders hanging in the mouth of horses that are fighting to leave the fence up is disheartening, to say the least!) Incidentally, when horses make extravagant jumps over *every* fence, it is usually a sign that they have been recently rapped, and this kind of extravagance is not likely to last forever. Making a ridiculously great effort over ordinary fences is highly unnatural, and horses that do it tend to "run out of gas" and enthusiasm very quickly. One has to suspend judgment on such horses until you can see what they look like under more normal conditions.

The question of how much scope or pure jumping ability you need is related to what you intend to do with the horse. A good rule of thumb is that the horse should be able to jump nine inches or a foot higher, in a pinch, than the average height of fences it will have to jump in competition. Junior horses and equitation horses that are going to spend their lives jumping three feet six inches and occasionally three feet nine inches ought to be able to jump four feet three inches to four feet six inches if they get there just right; show hunters ought to be able to jump four feet nine inches or five feet on a good day, speed horses at least five feet three inches, and so on. Of course, many will far exceed these minimums. Buddy Brown's equitation horse Sandsablaze graduated from the junior ranks with Buddy and went on to win the Grand Prix of Dublin and a gold medal in the Pan American Games, while Billy Haggard's Bold Minstrel, who started life as a show hunter *cum* Three-Day Event horse, held the puissance record in the old (Fiftieth Street) Madison Square Garden at seven feet three inches.

Grand Prix and Games horses are a law unto themselves. Though the clean jumper with ability in the six-foot range can win a lot of Grands Prix, really big scope (the ability to jump seven feet or more consistently) is an enormous advantage. Not only does it usually enable the horse to operate at lower levels of demand on its courage and basic ability; it also provides a wider margin for rider error. Nonetheless, in practice there is often a trade-off between scope and agility, and as today's courses again become lighter and more "technical" the careful, clever horse often finds the balance tipping back in its favor.

Any show horse also needs to have a good enough temperament to enable it to make optimum use of whatever other attributes it possesses. This will involve a reasonable degree of "ridability," a high level of courage or "nerve" and an ability to rise to big occasions under maximum pressure (and often, less than ideal physical circumstances). This is not at all the same thing as an *easy* temperament. Indeed, if you want the horse to take the course of most resistance with respect to not knocking down fences, it may well take a course of more resistance at various points in its training as well. My experience has been that the best horses have often been difficult to break as youngsters, and frequently grow up to have "difficult" temperaments in maturity, too. But then, so it is among people; one finds few "pussycats" among the overachievers.

It is regrettable that temperament, being so important, is also so difficult to evaluate at first glance. Many older horsemen depend a lot on the horse's general expression, and this may often be the secret of the "good eye for a horse." We're sometimes tempted to think of temperamental defects as being less immutable than physical problems, and there is some justification for this, for many behavioral defects can be improved or even cured through training and stable management, as discussed earlier. A lazy horse will always be lazy, but if you get it very fit and make it very responsive to the leg and the "cluck," you can conceal the problem from anyone who's not sitting on its back. A "hot" temperament can also be modified considerably through work, feed, turnout and riding, and some (like myself) even consider a touch of hot blood an advantage, provided that the boiling point is not *too* low.

The more serious temperamental defects, however, are just as bad as physical defects, and just as likely to be incorrigible. You can cover up a sulky or dishonest disposition for a while, but if the basic temperament is roguish or nappy (and the horse has already been gelded) it will probably go to the grave that way, no matter how skilled or patient the rider. The true lunatic and the real coward belong in the same category. You can modify their behavior to a point, but in the end their innate personality will out; they are time-wasters at best and menaces at worst, no matter how gifted. I might add that most of the riders I've seen badly hurt have been the victims of horses with bad temperaments rather than of horses lacking in ability.

It's a widespread belief (with which I agree) that temperament and breeding often go together, and that some breeds or races generally share more jumping ability than others. Even so, just as "no good horse is a bad color," no good jumper is of a bad breed. I have known good jumpers that were Quarter Horses, Palominos, Standardbreds, Appaloosas, Morgans, Arabians and American Saddlebreds, as well, of course, as all the traditional breeds, and every imaginable kind of mixture. Deep down inside, I think the Thoroughbred is the best equine athlete that has yet evolved. Nonetheless, even the Thoroughbred can sometimes benefit from an infusion of other blood with respect to size, substance and stability of temperament (especially these days, when Thoroughbred breeders seem to emphasize precocity and early speed above all else). Actually, there is so much Thoroughbred blood in many warmblood pedigrees today that the old distinctions have become very much blurred. My advice is to judge each horse on its individual merits and welcome an outstanding jumper no matter what sort of pedigree it happens to have.

A final consideration, perhaps less objective, is the suitability of the horse to the rider concerned. Very aggressive riders can do well with horses that would be anathema to riders who dislike creating all their own impulsion—and vice versa. Big riders look no more ridiculous on small horses than small riders look on big ones, not to mention the problem of putting your leg in the right place. "Flaky" horses get short shrift from riders who dislike playing psychoanalyst as well as jockey, while others (who may be rather free spirits themselves) can show them endless patience, and even develop considerable mutual confidence. Of course, really good riders should be resourceful enough to adapt to outstandingly talented horses of a type that might not otherwise be their first choice, just as the famous violinist Ysaÿe insisted that his pupils learn to play *the* violin, not only their own particular instrument. Even so, you'll always be happier with a horse that is physically and temperamentally suited to you, than with any marriage of convenience.

Looking back over the great horses I have seen, as well as the considerable number I have been privileged to ride, I am struck by their almost infinite variety of types, sizes, shapes and breeding origins. The only common denominators I can discern are that they were all strong personalities in their own ways; they all disliked hitting fences more than the average horse does (though not all to the same degree); and they all had enough physical equipment not to have to do so. None of them was an easy horse, and only a handful were really beautiful individuals, but they were outstandingly generous and tenacious, and could always seem to come up with an extra effort when in trouble. Finally, each one had as a collaborator a rider who really believed in its ability.

•   •   •

A few final words. Taking things for granted is all too easy. But we must never forget, every time we sit on a horse, what an extraordinary privilege it is: to be able to unite one's body with that of another sentient being, one that is stronger, faster and more agile by far than we are, and at the same time, brave, generous and uncommonly forgiving. (How much poorer our lives would be if all our riding experiences were restricted to mechanized transport!)

Only as riders can we achieve some measure of eternal youth, since we can exchange old, tired bodies for younger, more vigorous ones as easily as changing horses. Luckily, however, there is no surer antidote for the arrogance this circumstance might engender than the horse itself, for no poorer respecter of personages has ever existed. The horse doesn't know or care if you are prince or pauper, only whether you can ride with skill and justness. No throne can compare with the back of a horse, and there is no way in which man can come closer to nature than by becoming one with a horse. Truly, as the French like to say, *"L'homme se complete par le cheval,"* "Man completes himself through the horse." Nobody has ever understood and articulated this better than Shakespeare:

> *When I bestride him, I soar, I am a hawk;*
> *He trots the air, the earth sings when he touches it . . .*

—Henry V, *Act III*

SELECTED BIBLIOGRAPHY

*T*his is not intended as a "show-off" bibliography, but is a small selection of serious and valuable books that are all in English, and all either still in print or fairly readily available. (Good sources are Miller's, 235 Murray Hill Parkway, East Rutherford, NJ 07073, for current books, and J. A. Allen & Co., 1 Lower Grosvenor Place, London SW1 OEL, England, and Bucephalus Books, P.O. Box 380, Long Valley, NJ 07853, for anything published on horses since 1550.) I have read all of these books and consulted them many times, for there is no better way to work out of a dead end in your thinking than to see what some experienced horsemen have had to say about

153

your problem. If you don't yet have an equestrian library to consult, these books would make a good starting point.

Books dealing primarily with equitation on the flat or dressage:

Decarpentry, General A. E. *Academic Equitation.* London: J. A. Allen, 1979.

Jousseaume, André. *Progressive Dressage.* London: J. A. Allen, 1978.

Paillard, Jean Saint-Fort. *Understanding Horsemanship.* Garden City, N.Y.: Doubleday, 1977.

Podhajsky, Alois. *The Complete Training of Horse and Rider.* Garden City, N.Y.: Doubleday, 1967.

Seunig, Waldemar. *Horsemanship.* Garden City, N.Y.: Doubleday, 1969.

Books that deal with jumping as well:

Blixen-Finecke, Hans von. *The Art of Riding.* London: J. A. Allen, 1977.

Chamberlin, Brigadier General Harry D. *Training Hunters, Jumpers and Hacks.* New York: Arco, 1972.

Endrödy, Lieutenant Colonel Agoston d'. *Give Your Horse a Chance.* London: J. A. Allen, 1971.

Klimke, Reiner. *Basic Training of the Young Horse.* London: J. A. Allen, 1985.

Licart, Commandant Jean. *Basic Equitation.* New York: Arco, 1972.

Müseler, Wilhelm. *Riding Logic.* New York: Arco, 1984.

Némethy, Bertalan de. *The De Némethy Method.* New York: Doubleday, 1988.

About the Author

Bill Steinkraus first attracted the attention of the equestrian world by winning both national equitation championships in 1941. After a stint in Burma with the 124th Cavalry Regiment and graduation from Yale, he resumed his competitive career in the late 1940s and in 1951 earned a place on the first "civilian" Olympic show jumping team. For the next twenty-two years Steinkraus was a mainstay of the Team, and was named to six Olympic teams.

Though an injury to his horse in 1964 limited his Olympic appearances to five, Steinkraus won four Olympic medals, including the first individual show jumping gold ever won by an American, in 1968. He also rode on thirty-nine winning Nations' Cup teams, and won over one hundred individual international competitions, including the coveted George V Gold Cup (twice), the International Championship of Germany and the Grands Prix of London, Rotterdam, Ostend (three times), Toronto (five times) and New York (twice), among others.

A member of the Show Jumping, National Horse Show, Madison Square Garden and New York Sports Halls of Fame, Steinkraus became president of the U.S. Equestrian Team after retiring from international competition in 1972, and is currently its chairman. He is also a member of the Bureau and Chairman of the World Cup Committee of the International Equestrian Federation (FEI), and a widely experienced international jumping judge.

Married to a noted dressage judge and rider, Helen, he is the father of three sons, and still rides every day whenever he is at home in Connecticut. His previous books include *Riding and Jumping, The Complete Book of Show Jumping, The USET Book of Riding* and *The Horse in Sport.*